# The Evangel

# God's Power

# for Salvation

Don Bast

ISBN:1496172477

ISBN-13:9781496172471

## DEDICATION

This book is dedicated to the one I love, my wife Marja. She has been a constant source of inspiration for over 43 years. She is not only the primary proofreader of this book and much of my work but she is my main mentor and harshest critic, also. The Lord knew I would need her in this area and in too many others to mention. By His amazing grace, we have survived and continue to slowly but surely grow together in the realization of God.

## NOTE TO THE READER

All Bible passages quoted in this writing are taken from the Concordant Literal Version unless otherwise stated.

# CONTENTS

Don Bast

# INTRODUCTION

Many years ago, I heard a preacher make this statement, "I would rather the saints of God **understand grace and not live it** than to **not understand grace yet live it**." What he meant by the term "live it", was to live a good, clean life, pleasing to the Lord. He went on to explain that these two opposing positions are the two main tendencies to which Christians are bent. The first group that "understands grace" believes their **salvation is 100% a gracious gift from God** and thus reasons that since they did nothing to win God's favor, there is no merit in being concerned with trying to live a holy life.

To be fair to the preacher; he did not say that the status of this group was ideal. He simply stated that their position was better than that of the other group, who did "not understand grace", therefore were striving to live a holy life, thinking that it is **their own righteousness that earns their salvation.** His claim was that they were working to gain something that had already been gratuitously granted to them, when they first believed.

My goal is to extract from each of these two contrasting views what is true and real. We will then use our findings as a springboard to launch towards further truth based on God's word, and especially from the apostle Paul's epistles.

First of all, I must add that I can totally relate to the preacher's assessment of the different positions. From the age of 22, and well into my 40's I lived in religious bondage attempting to win God's favor by my good works. Over time, as I grew in the realization of grace, my heart was set free, from those shackles. However, as is often the case, when a pendulum swings too far in one direction, it naturally does the same in the opposite direction; so it was with my experience. The next two decades I spent enjoying life and God's grace while wasting much time and energy, simply using my freedom in Christ for an occasion or *an incentive to the flesh* (Galatians 5:13).

During this period, I traveled long distances, several times a year, to conferences in different cities, where others of like faith were gathered. Birds of a feather flock together! I thoroughly enjoyed these meetings, gained much scriptural knowledge, made some lasting friendships and will always be thankful for this special time in my life.

However, there was one thing that was not ideal about these gatherings and relationships; they seemed to foster in me a growing tendency to look down on other believers. Those who didn't share the same revelation of grace and freedom as we did were often scorned and even ridiculed. Pride filled my heart as I gloried in the fact that God chose us, His select few, to receive these wonderful revelations. But it started to bother me that I couldn't enjoy fellowship with other believers, even those who were sincerely serving the Lord, but didn't see the truth as I did. I hated the wall between us but was clueless on how to even begin to remove it.

Periodically comments were made that we were spending too much time preaching to the choir and that we were becoming little more than a group of "think tanks". Like the Athenians, of the first century, we were **unusually religious** (Acts 17:22), especially when it came to studying the scriptures. Unfortunately, I'm afraid the motivation for many of us was becoming more and more like *"the Athenians and their foreign visitors who used to **devote their whole leisure to telling or hearing about something new**"* (:21, Weymouth).

Mainly because of our strong emphasis, on the importance of having correct doctrine, a sectarian spirit found a way to flourish in our midst. We were taught that bad behavior not doctrine was the only valid reason to separate from other believers and we should have known better. However, the differences caused an increasing contention and the group finally split into several factions with each going their separate way. Some of the conferences continue, amongst these smaller groups, each focusing on their pet teachings.

I say all this, only to affirm that I sincerely empathize with both positions, the preacher identified, because I have spent long periods in both camps. I was not a mere bystander, either. I have passionately pursued both extremes on my long journey toward the "Promised Land". I often refer to this 40-year period, of my life, as God's direct route through the wilderness.

As I look back at these two very different times and approaches to "living for God", I have to agree with the preacher's assessment. From my experience, even **a vague understanding of grace**, which causes one to become apathetic, is still preferable to the condemnation I wallowed in, never being able to live up to the high standard of God's law. I don't think my opinion is an isolated one, either. Others I met in this latter group came from similar religious backgrounds. The natural inclination, for many who labored long and hard attempting to "crucify the flesh" and to "take up their cross daily", in order to stay saved, or to endure to the end, seems to be a pull towards anything that looks like freedom, especially under the guise of understanding grace.

For a time, at least, after so many years of spiritual bondage, it was so refreshing to be able to relax and just enjoy the simple pleasures of life again. However, more and more, I was sensing an uneasiness in my spirit and the Lord began to put a hunger in my heart to know Him in a deeper measure. He showed me that my spiritual journey was not over; I had not arrived yet. He also revealed to me that as enjoyable as my life was, I was spinning my spiritual wheels, going nowhere fast. If I was to go on to maturity, I realized that some day, I must face the critical issue that even though all may be allowed me, all is not expedient, practical or edifying (1Corinthians 10:23).

I had to admit that by using my freedom in Christ, as an excuse to continue living according to the flesh something inside was slowly dying (Romans 8:13). It started to bother me that there was little, of lasting value, being accomplished in my life. I began to be haunted by two questions; "How much good am I doing those I love?" And more importantly, "Was my life really glorifying God and His gospel?" It was humbling, but I had to admit the error of my way, once again. It seems some of us have to learn so many lessons in life the hard way. But what is the alternative? Is ignorance really bliss? Of course not!

*Are you not aware that to whom you are presenting yourselves as slaves for obedience, his slaves you are, whom you are obeying, whether of Sin for death, or of Obedience for righteousness?* (Romans 6:16).

Finally and thankfully, I am coming to realize that although this principle applies to all mankind, it was specifically written to believers, for our admonition.

## Legalism and Pure Grace Fatalism

For the sake of this writing I will label these two positions, which are really two different spiritual life-styles, as "legalism" and "pure grace fatalism". Of course God's grace is pure, as this writing will confirm. The term "pure grace" will be used only to identify the one group of believers the preacher mentioned. Even though few would  readily adopt either handle as their own, the tendency for God's people, to be drawn in one direction or the other appears to be a universal phenomenon. Those who claim to "understand grace" often become **fatalistic** and, or **apathetic**. Those who do "not understand grace" tend to become **legalistic**, for a time at least.

One or the other of the extremes seems difficult to avoid, especially for us who spent our childhood under the instruction of, what many refer to as, "Bible thumpers" and or "holiness preachers". I grew up on the front pew of a Conservative Mennonite mission church. At an early age I learned to fear God and the fires of hell. When one is subjected, at such an impressionable time, to this form of "spiritual abuse", a lasting mark is branded on the mind. As a sheer matter of survival and sanity, it seems inevitable to seek refuge in one camp or the other.

"Legalism" according to Webster's dictionary is " the doctrine of salvation by good works". Most every sect will adamantly deny that they promote legalism. They admit that each denomination has a unique focus on certain doctrines and that their creeds and traditions differ somewhat. But when it is all said and done, almost without exception they all teach that in order to be saved and to stay saved one **must do something.** Some groups claim that something as simple as infant baptism is all that is necessary. Others teach that water baptism as an adult or keeping the Sabbath is essential for salvation; many groups include other things such as tithing, communion etc, and the list goes on.

There are however, some who make the claim that all one has to do to be saved is to believe certain doctrines, in your heart, and confess them openly with your mouth. In fact, this is the exercise that qualifies for membership in many churches, also. Once this is accomplished members must keep the faith until they die to be assured a ticket to heaven and to enjoy their "eternal security" along the way. This is what I mean when I use the term "legalism".

Webster defines "fatalism" as "the belief that all events are determined by fate and are hence inevitable". Christian fatalism or pure grace fatalism at least gives God the credit for determining the outcome of all events, which I do also. The Deity of God and the Sovereignty of Christ is another vast topic, maybe for another writing. However, there is a fatalism that says, "When it comes to God's grand purpose or intention and also His will for my personal life, "**whatever will be, will be**; regardless of what I believe or what I do; whether I pray or not, God has predetermined how every detail will unfold". This kind of fatalism leads to apathy, which Webster defines as "lack of interest; listless condition; unconcern; indifference." The scriptures do not teach this. There are many things God has determined will come to pass because we pray. He has also determined to accomplish certain things through us, and He will therefore lead us, and empower us, accordingly. The point is, He wants us involved. He has purposed to work in us and use us as His instruments, to accomplish His intention, for His glory.

Legalism and pure grace fatalism are both deceptions of the Adversary. Frankly our enemy is not particular which one we prefer as long as one, or the other, keeps us from growing in the realization of God. Both are a mixture of part truth and part error; one errs on the side of caution and unbelief and the other on the side of license and liberty. One is an **active denial** of the truth; the other is a **passive denial**. The truth of the evangel, which is the power of God for salvation, is squarely realized far above and beyond these two lies; it is discovered only **in grace, through faith**.

Before we go further, consider this question, "Is it possible that these opposing tendencies are flip sides of the same counterfeit coin, systematically staged against each other, in order to distract us from what is true and real?" After investigating each position extensively I know, for sure, neither is ideal and neither is in accord with a realization of *the grace of God in truth*. (Colossians 1:6). As is often the case, with opposing views, and especially, with opposing doctrines, there is a **third option**, which is closer to the truth. This is the direction we trust God will lead. May His spirit pour in us a love for the truth, even if it hurts, humbles or exposes our preconceived notions and faulty doctrines, for what they are? Many of us have much "unlearning" to do. As the light gets brighter, the scales will fall from our eyes. The shackles that bound us will be broken, one by one, as the truth, line upon line, makes us free.

## Understanding Grace but Not Living It

Besides not being ideal or even desirable, let me suggest that both positions stated by the preacher are actually not even possible. Perhaps most readers will more readily agree, that without at least, a basic understanding of God's saving grace and faith in Jesus Christ, one cannot be saved or even begin to live a life pleasing to God. It seems to me that those interested in this writing probably already understand that *by works of law, no flesh at all shall be justified in God's sight* (Romans 3:20, Galatians 2:16). Regardless of how we personally interpret, what the preacher meant by, "living it", I think most will agree that this is impossible without some realization of grace. Regardless, we must go on.

Some may not be as receptive to the idea that the other position, "understanding grace and not living it" is impossible, also. This matter will become a focal point of this writing. My prayer is that an honest look at the scriptures will reveal to any seeker of truth that it is impossible to really understand grace and not live a life pleasing to God. I have come to believe that, as assuredly as it is true that without the power of God, and His grace, **we cannot "live it",** the opposite is also true. Simply stated, with the reality of grace, daily operating in our heart**, we cannot, not "live it".** Let me suggest that these two facts are also the flip sides of the same truth?

## From the Day

In the following verses, which precede the passage known as the "Colossian prayer" a basic truth regarding the connection between grace and pleasing God is revealed.

*You hear before in* **the word of truth of the evangel,** (A.V. gospel) *which, being present with you, according as in the entire world also, is bearing fruit and growing, according as it is among you also, from the day on which you hear and realized the grace of God in truth (Colossians 1:5,6).*

This clear declaration of God reveals that **from the day** one hears the evangel and **realizes the grace of God in truth** he or she will bear fruit. When the word **is present**, and *remains with you* (Weymouth) it will begin to grow.

Let me suggest that not only is this true but also, to the degree that the word remains and one grows in the realization of grace, and God's will, in all wisdom and spiritual understanding, (:9), to the same degree he or she will instinctively be walking *worthily of the Lord, for all pleasing, bearing fruit in every good work* (:10). As we grow in the realization of God and His grace, bearing fruit and walking worthily is the joyous, natural result.

In the parable of the sower of Matthew 13, this truth is confirmed. Jesus said this about the seed that fell beside the road, "*coming is the wicked one and **snatching what has been sown in his heart**"* (:19). The seed that fell on the rocky ground He said, *"this is he who is hearing the word and straightway with joy **is** getting it, yet has **no root in himself**, but is temporary. Now at the coming of affliction or persecution because of the word, **he is snared**"(:20,21).* That being sown amongst the thorns, *"is he who is hearing the word, and the worry of this eon and the seduction of riches are **stifling the word**, and it is becoming **unfruitful**"* (:22). And lastly, that being sown on the ideal earth, *" is he who is hearing the word and understanding, who by all means is bearing fruit, and is producing; these indeed, a hundred, yet these sixty, yet these thirtyfold"* (:23).

This fact is a primary truth  in accord with the gospel or "the evangel", which we will call it in this writing. '"The term **evangel** is much preferred to "gospel", as it has the verb **evangelize** and the noun **evangelist** in accepted usage and it is not encumbered with many unscriptural associations and phrases."' (Concordant Literal Keyword, pg. 93)

Regardless of the title given, it remains the good news, literally WELL-MESSAGE, centered around the fact that Christ died for our sins according to the scriptures, and that He was entombed, and that He has been roused the third day according to the scriptures (1Corinthians 15:3,4).

The evangel is the message that, first and foremost, reveals the heart of our loving Father and glorifies His Beloved Son. This message is God's power for salvation. Before we specifically look at the evangel let me confirm one point. Although, we cannot bear fruit or create any amount of growth in our  own strength; we are not mere by-standers. We are dramatically involved in this life long, on-going, wonderful process. If we believe the good news and love its truth  nothing can prevent us from walking worthily and bearing fruit, in grace through faith.

The many aspects of walking worthily and bearing fruit will be a prominent part of this writing. For now let us look at an entreaty by the apostle Paul, which identifies some primary elements of a worthy walk.

*I am entreating you, then, I, the prisoner in the Lord, to walk worthily of the calling with which you were called, with all* **humility** *and* **meekness,** *with* **patience,** *bearing with one another in* **love,** *endeavoring to keep the* **unity** *of the spirit with the tie of* **peace** (Ephesians 4:1-3).

Love is the one sign, above all others, of walking worthily. It will be demonstrated by humility, meekness and unity. The many denominations, divisions, sects and strife boldly attest to the fact that we, as a people, have fallen far short of a walking in a manner pleasing to the Lord. This is a tell-tale sign that God's grace has not yet overwhelmed us, as a whole, *with faith and love,* (1Timothy 1:14). At the very least we have not grown to maturity in the realization of grace.

Our primary motive in presenting this conclusion is not to point fingers, but to agree with God's word and to open the door of our hearts to allow His grace to reign in us in a greater measure. May we as individuals not be guilty of underestimating the power of grace, in our own life by shunning the numerous entreaties to *walk worthily of the calling with which we were called* (Ephesians 4:1). Instead, let us continue to pray together with one mind,

*That the God of our Lord Jesus Christ, the Father of glory, may be giving us a spirit of wisdom and revelation in the realization of Him, the eyes of our heart having been enlightened, for us to*

*perceive what is the expectation of His calling, and the riches of the glory of the enjoyment of His allotment among the saints, and the transcendent greatness of His power for us who are believing, in accord with the operation of the might of His strength* (Ephesians 1:17-19).

God, the Father of glory, has given His children a spirit of wisdom and revelation for specific reasons. The eyes of our heart have been enlightened to enable us to comprehend the **expectation of His calling**, and the **riches of the glory** of what is prepared for us. There is more; God, at this time, is revealing to His saints the supreme **greatness of His power** for us who believe His evangel. May our continual prayer be that this power would be operating in us daily, as we grow in our understanding and the realization of grace?

This writing is in no way meant to be an exhaustive study on this vast subject and neither do I claim to be capable of providing such. Our goal is to simply bring attention to some vital issues and to spur on a few at least  to study God's word on their own. Spiritual wisdom cannot be learned it must be revealed by the sprit. It is not wise to blindly accept this writing or any other regardless how impressive it may sound.

Let me clarify one thought, at the outset; we are not contending for mere doctrines in our pursuit for truth. Deep in the heart of all God's children is an aching, a longing to know Him. We are all craving a living message that will reveal His character and a spiritual light that will dissolve the gloomy clouds of man's theology that has kept His face hidden for too long.

Surely, if we are honest we will admit that we, God's "called out people", have left our "**first love**" and have all but lost "**the joy of the Lord**". Together let us contend for the faith once given to the saints; that of being **set apart for Him alone**. He will provide the grace, wisdom, and power as we dedicate ourselves to know Him. We will never be fully satisfied until we can openly justify Him and honor Him in the presence of our enemies.

The scriptures speak of a message as a living demonstration of spirit and power, a truth above all else, too marvelous to be hid any longer. Those who seek this treasure, with their whole heart, shall surely find it. It has been hidden in God, all along and can be found in His living word, through a fresh revelation of the good news message of the grace of God.

O foolish Legalists! *Who bewitches you? . . . This only I want to learn from you: Did you get the spirit by works of law or by hearing of faith? So foolish are you? Undertaking in spirit, are you now being completed in flesh?* (Galatians 3:1-3).

O foolish "Pure Grace" believers! Who bewitches you? Did you get the spirit by learning doctrine or by hearing of faith? So foolish are you? Beginning in spirit are you now completed by rightly aligning all your doctrinal ducks in a row?

We have heard the word of truth, the evangel of our salvation, we believed and were sealed with the holy spirit of promise. As glorious as this is, it is the beginning not the end; it is the earnest of the enjoyment of our allotment. There is so much more to discover, to experience and to enjoy.

# CHAPTER 1

# The Evangel of the Grace of God

## The Apostle Paul

*Saul, breathing out threatening and murder against the disciples of the Lord, approaching the chief priest, requests from him letters for Damascus to the synagogues, so that, if he should be finding any who are of the way, both men and women, he may be leading them bound to Jerusalem* (Acts 9:1,2).

Traveling on the Damascus Road, hunting down and threatening with murder the disciples of the Lord, Saul of Tarsus, was himself apprehended by the risen, glorified Christ, the very One he was persecuting. A bright light, out of heaven, flashed about him, (:3) there and then he was literally knocked off of his religious high-horse (:4) and was blinded for three days (:9). When his natural eyesight returned; his whole outlook and purpose in life was drastically altered. God stopped him in his tracks and informed him that he was His choice instrument (AV chosen vessel) (:15). Saul, later called Paul (13:9) was the man God hand-picked to proclaim the good news of Christ crucified, the same message he had been working tirelessly to wipe out.

*Faithful is the saying, and worthy of all welcome, that Christ Jesus came into the world to save sinners, foremost of whom am I. But therefore was I shown mercy, that in me, the foremost, Jesus Christ should be displaying all His patience, for a pattern of those who are about to be believing on Him for life eonian* [life of the Ages, Weymouth]  (1Timothy 1:15,16).

Paul's life was immediately and completely transformed. Not only did he become the pattern or model of God's saving grace but God also revealed to him a secret that had, up until this time, been completely hidden to mankind.

*Paul, the prisoner of Christ Jesus for you, the nations since you surely hear of the administration of the grace of God that is given to me for you, for by revelation the secret is made known to me* (Ephesians 3:1-3).

Christ Jesus our Lord, deemed Paul faithful, and assigned him this special service and also invigorated him to accomplish it. Henceforth, he dedicated all his energies to fulfill this assignment, to herald (make known publicly with authority, Concordant keyword, pg. 143) the evangel of the glory of the happy God (1Timothy 1:11,12). Upon receiving the revelation of the grace of God and his mission, the apostle Paul immediately became consumed with his calling and service and made this vow.

*I am not making my soul precious to myself, till I should be perfecting my career and the dispensation, which I got from the Lord Jesus, to certify the evangel of the grace of God* (Acts 20:24).

This would not be an easy task, to say the least. The apostle Paul endured years of almost unbelievable hardship and persecution **because of the evangel**. He remained faithful to the end and shortly before his death penned these words,

*I am already a libation, and the period of my dissolution is imminent. I have contended the ideal contest. I have finished my career. I have kept the faith. Furthermore, there is reserved for me the wreath of righteousness, which the Lord, the just Judge, will be paying to me in that day; yet not to me only, but also to all who love His advent* (2Timothy 4:6-8).

## The Word of the Cross

*Not ashamed am I of the evangel, for it is God's power for salvation to everyone who is believing* (Romans 1:16).

**The evangel**, the good news given to this servant of God almost 2000 years ago, is still **God's power for salvation today**, to everyone who believes it.

*The word of the cross is stupidity, indeed, to those who are perishing, yet to us who are being saved it is the power of God* (1Corinthians1:18).

The heart of the evangel of God is synonymous with the word of the cross. One is said to be **God's power** the other **the power of God**. The message itself is power for salvation.

*We are heralding Christ crucified, to Jews, indeed, a snare, yet to the nations stupidity, yet to those who are called, both Jews and Greeks, Christ, the power of God and the wisdom of God* (:23,24).

This simple but powerful message of Christ crucified, and God's amazing grace, is so misunderstood, even by many who claim to believe it. This sad fact only makes the power and the **glory inherent in the evangel** that much more precious for those who see it and love it with all their heart. Those who truly realize the grace of God in truth enjoy a steadfast faith, anchored in God that is impossible otherwise and yet remains hidden to most of the world around them.

## Obtaining God's Power for Salvation

The truth about Christ crucified and the power of the grace of God for salvation is not complicated. It is simple enough for a child to understand, but not unlike all of God's truths it cannot be learned it must be revealed to an open, hungry heart. When speaking of God's revelation truth the apostle Paul declared,

*That which is of God no one knows, except the spirit of God. We are speaking, not with words taught by human wisdom, but with those taught by the spirit, matching spiritual blessings with spiritual words* (1Corinthians 2:11,13).

Only the holy spirit, which the Father gives to those who believe, is able to teach us all we need to know (John 14:26). All spiritual truth is only for those who have God's spirit making its home in them. *If anyone has not Christ's spirit, this one is not His* (Romans 8:9). Unless Christ's spirit reveals it men will not, nay cannot even see it, let alone obtain the power. It is only for those who believe the message. To them the evangel itself is the power of God for salvation.

Let us first consider the nature and the content of the good news message. We begin our study by focusing our attention on one sentence from Ephesians. Here we find listed several simple but profound and comprehensive statements, regarding this glorious topic. To be able to receive the love of the truth, in these two short verses, is to enter into the joy of our salvation.

*In grace, through faith, are you saved, and this is not out of you; it is God's approach present, not of works, lest anyone should be boasting* (Ephesians 2:8,9).

Understandably, the whole concept of being **saved in grace**, or by any other method, will have little appeal to unbelievers, those ruled by their senses and not by the spirit.

*The soulish man* (AV natural man) *is not receiving the things, which are of the spirit of God, for they are stupidity to him, and he is not able to know them* (1Corinthians 2:14).

Those of us who do believe can appreciate this fact, by recalling the days when we were in the same boat, with no interest in spiritual matters. On the other hand, it is quite disturbing to realize that many who name the name of Christ are not able to take this clear and simple declaration at face value. These words are meant to be refreshing words of life to a weary soul.

The sound of the Father's heart of love resonates through the words *"in grace you are saved* and *this is not out of you"*. They portray the Saviour's arms open wide. The invitation is, *Come to Me* [as you are] *all burdened ones and I will give you rest, for my yoke is easy, and my burden is ligh*t (Matthew 11:28-30).

The only reason I can imagine why a believer in Christ Jesus seeking for truth would not comprehend and cheerfully embrace this clear statement is that their heart has been blinded and hardened by the creeds of Christendom and false doctrines of demons. Today's "man-centered gospel" has reasoned away and all but rendered void these powerful words of spirit and life. And in doing so, has single-handedly brought more shame to the character of God and the truth about His ways than all other human philosophy.

Regardless of how many refuse and deny it or how few we are who believe what is written here we are obligated to *let God be true, yet every man* [who contradicts] *a liar* (Romans 3:4). These are spiritual words in accord with the evangel of the grace of God.

## Five Easy Pieces

Let us break down our main text into five easy pieces in order to examine in the simplest of terms how one is saved. The **first**, primary element listed here is the fact that it is **in grace** we are saved. Salvation takes place in the sphere of grace. We will look at the meaning of grace in depth, shortly. The **second** element is that salvation is **through faith**. Faith is the medium or the vehicle that delivers the realization or reality of our salvation. We will presently look closer at faith, also. **Thirdly**, our salvation, including our faith, the act of believing, is **not out of us**. It did not originate in us. **Fourthly**, we see that our salvation was actually **God's present**, a gift graciously granted to us. Paul reinforces this truth by adding a **fifth** phrase, **not of works**. Salvation has nothing to do with anything we did or could do.

Immediately after the basis of salvation is established, Paul also provides an explanation why God decided that it was to be this way. The reason we are saved in grace through faith is **lest anyone should be boasting**. This gift is so precious to us and to God Himself that He will not allow it to be sullied by man's involvement, whatsoever. He left no room for us to take any credit for our salvation lest anyone should attempt to rob God of His glory by boasting in himself.

## Grace is Grace, Nothing Less

There is no doubt that almost every student of the scriptures, and every believer in Christ Jesus, will make reference to their need, of what the Bible calls grace. It would be unthinkable to do otherwise. However, saying or writing the word grace does not make it grace. Like Israel as a nation, so Christendom as an organized religion, stumbles over the foolishness of the sacrifice of Christ, the spotless lamb, in the giving of His life for their sins and the sins of the whole world. They may deny it in word but their actions prove that they like Israel are pursuing a righteousness through law, albeit their own custom-made set of creeds, rules and regulations. Therefore the result is the same.

*Wherefore? Seeing that it is not out of faith, but as out of law works, they stumble on the stumbling stone* (Romans 9:32).

*They being ignorant of the righteousness of God, and seeking to establish their own righteousness, are not subjected to the righteousness of God. For Christ is the consummation of law for righteousness to everyone believing* (Romans 10:3,4).

For centuries multitudes have been lured into a perpetual systematic performance of religious rituals and, or following the creeds and traditions of man instead of looking to Jesus alone, *the author and perfecter of faith* (Hebrews 12:2, Young's Literal). In doing so, one cannot be subject to Christ or to God's righteousness.

Although, Paul was entrusted to take the evangel of the grace of God to the nations (Galatians 2:7,8), he made it clear that not all Israel was set aside. Speaking of his brethren according to the flesh he makes an important observation that applies to all.

*Thus, then, in the current era also, there has come to be a remnant according to the choice of grace. Now if it is in grace, it is no longer out of works, else the grace is coming to be no longer grace. Now, if it is out of works, it is no longer grace, else the work is no longer work* (Romans 11:5,6).

For Jew and Gentile alike, in this administration of the grace of God, (Ephesians 3:2) there is one way to get saved; it is in grace. We must see grace as it is, or else God's truths and operations will become veiled, even for the most sincere believer.

## The Glory of Grace

*He Himself has declared, "I am Yahweh! (Jehovah) That is My name, and I will not give My glory to another"* (Isaiah 42:8).

God actually chose us in Christ *before the disruption of the world, we to be holy and flawless in His sight, in love designating us beforehand for the place of a son for Him through Christ Jesus; in accord with the delight of His will, for the laud* (applause) *of the glory of His grace, which graces us in the Beloved* (Ephesians 1:4-6).

God's motive in choosing us, designating us to be sons and saving us is for the applause of the **glory of His grace**. To remove all doubt, about the nature and source of salvation it is written, *"this is **not out of you**; it is **God's approach present**"*. Like all God's gifts, when it comes to our salvation, not one

*Gives to Him first, and it will be repaid him, seeing that out of Him and through Him and for Him is all: to Him be the glory for the eons! Amen* (Romans 11:35,36).

The term "approach present" refers back to certain animal sacrifices offered up to God by the Jewish priests of old. A study of the book of Leviticus would surely add insight into the term but there is also one familiar reference in Matthew's gospel account that will suffice. Here we see the gold, frankincense and myrrh offered by the three Magi to the babe in the manger are called approach presents (Matthew 2:11).

Every aspect of salvation, including justification, which we will discuss later, is as free as sunshine and the air we breathe. Even our faith is *graciously granted* to us*, for Christ's sake* (Philippians 1:29). We cannot boast in the fact that we believed God or the evangel when His grace overwhelmed us *with faith and love in Christ Jesus* (1Timothy 1:14).

"Faith creates nothing, does nothing, deserves nothing, and has no efficacy apart from its Object, for it is *not* a saviour. If I entrust myself to an elevator that I may reach the tenth floor I contribute nothing to the power that raises me, nor does my ignorance of the mechanism prevent my being elevated to that floor." (George Rogers, Studies in Romans, p. 34)

In fact, the gracious gifts of God are tarnished the moment we connect them to any hint of merit or work. No one could pay the price for their salvation, justification or faith. They are all absolutely free. God will not be indebted to anyone; this is why we are **saved in grace**. When we are transported to glory and gaze into our Saviour's loving eyes, we will joyfully give Him all the credit for arriving safely.

## Access into Grace

Paul, in his writing to the ecclesia at Rome, expounds on the term **in grace through faith.** Before he does though, he first qualifies the kind of faith he is referring to; in other words, what one needs to believe in. It may go without saying, but allow me to make the point clear. Believing in a deaf and dumb idol, made out of wood, gold or silver, which is nothing, (1Corinthians 8:4) will not help or save anyone, from anything. Neither is it written that we must believe in a God who saves the religious or the law abiding or those smart enough to accept His Son as their personal Saviour. Instead it is written,

*To him who is not working, yet is believing on Him, Who is justifying the irreverent, his faith is reckoned for righteousness* (Romans 4:5).

Then in the next chapter he confirms the connection between grace and this kind of faith or believing.

*Being, then, justified by faith, we may be having peace toward God, through our Lord, Jesus Christ, through Whom we have the access also, by faith, into this grace in which we stand* (Romans 5:2).

Here it is revealed that through faith alone can we obtain **access into** the **grace** in which we stand. When God opens the eyes of our heart through faith, we will then understand that in God's mind and intention He saved us while we were **helpless, infirm, irreverent sinners**. This is salvation in grace.

*While we are still infirm, still in accord with the era, for the sake of the irreverent, Christ died. For hardly for the sake of a just man will anyone be dying: for, for the sake of a good man, perhaps someone may even be daring to die, yet God is commending this love of His to us, seeing that, **while we are still sinners**, Christ died for our sakes* (Romans 5:6-8).

This is the faith that provides free and glorious access into God's grace. Salvation from beginning to end is *of faith that it may accord with grace* (Romans 4:16).

Our **faith** does not save us; it **opens the eyes of our heart** to see what is freely given to us. Faith is the key that unlocks the door to allow us entry into the glorious realm of grace where we are saved. We do not initiate or manufacture faith on our own. The unseen spirit of God working in us gives us faith to believe and opens our eyes to see what is otherwise invisible.

*That which is of God no one knows, except the spirit of God. We obtained, not the spirit of the world, but the spirit which is of God, **that we may be perceiving that which is being graciously given to us by God*** (1Corinthians 2:11,12).

The spirit is freely given to us, to open the eyes of our heart, to perceive this gracious gift, of *free grace, which He bestowed on*

*us in Christ Jesus before the commencement of the Ages*
(2Timothy 1:9, Weymouth). The whole process takes place in
the sphere where grace operates. Only in grace is there
salvation. This simple truth is a fundamental fact of the evangel
of God and sets it apart from all other teachings, and all false
religions, and all other gospels, falsely so called.  In this good
news message alone is **God's righteousness revealed.**

*For not ashamed am I of the evangel, for it is God's power for*
*salvation to everyone who is believing - to the Jew first, and to*
*the Greek as well. For in it God's righteousness is being revealed*
*out of faith for faith* (Romans 1:16,17).

## Traditional Definitions of Grace

Two definitions of grace I learned growing up in the Mennonite
church were, "**unmerited favor** to the **unworthy**" and "**favor**
rendered to those who **deserve the opposite**". These are both
true statements but they are incomplete and flawed. They are
based on, and designed for a man-centered gospel. The word
"unmerited" is not necessary;  favor infers unmerited. The more
serious problem is in the fact that it refers to the unworthy
sinner. We have no place in a simple definition of grace.

Actually, the only part we play in grace is that which is similar to
the part man played in the crucifixion. When it came to the
death of Christ, man was necessary, to play the role of the
murderer and nothing more. Similarly, when it comes to grace,
in order for there to be a need of a Saviour, in the first place,
there needs to be sinners. This is the extent of our involvement
in the operation of grace. The favor is **from God, through Christ**
and **for His glory**. The attention should be primarily on Him.

Also, by adding more terms like "to the unworthy" and "those who deserve the opposite" the attention is firmly fastened on ourselves and thereby keeps our eyes off God our Saviour and the intended meaning. The power and beauty of God's grace is a display of His character and His righteousness. Worthiness or unworthiness, on our part, does not enter the equation of God's dealings with mankind. We cannot influence God's love for us! He already loves us more than we can apprehend. **He cannot love us more** than He already does.

Neither can we win God's favor or influence Him to give us anything or do anything for us! He has already given us His most precious possession, His Beloved Son. He has purposed and is in the process of blessing us beyond anything we could ever ask for or even comprehend.

*Surely, He Who spares not His own Son, but gives Him up for us all, how shall He not, together with Him, also, be **graciously granting us all**?* (Romans 8:32).

Entering into the realm where grace operates is the only way to get saved. Dwelling there is God's prescribed way to enjoy all He has for us; all that our heart desires. And here alone is  where we will discover the power to get hold of life, really.

# CHAPTER 2

## A Simple Message So Misunderstood

### Passages that Contradict?

One reason why the passages revealing the absolute power and glory of grace are misunderstood and discounted is due to the fact that there are other verses that appear to contradict. The following is a good example.

*I am making known to you, brethren, the evangel which I bring to you, which also you accepted, in which also you stand,* **through which also you are saved, if** *you are retaining what I said in bringing the evangel to you, outside and except you believe feignedly [not sincerely]* (1Corinthians 15:1,2).

In light of what we have said so far, what do we do with a statement that declares **we are saved if we do something**? Obviously just ignoring it is not an option and we will address this question shortly. We will also consider other similar passages and give close attention to the passage beginning with Philippians 2:12, *"With fear and trembling, be carrying your own salvation into effect".* (*work out your own salvation,* A. V.)

These conditional passages appear to contradict our main text from Ephesians 2:8,9 and what we have said so far about being saved in grace. The legalist and the fatalist alike are forced to cling to a certain set of verses and disregard the others in order to substantiate their erroneous doctrines. It is foolish to be satisfied with a half-truth, turning a blind eye to the other side of what is written.

We will sincerely attempt to face both sides of this paradox. We cannot be afraid of the truth. Our confidence is not in having a neatly packaged set of doctrines. Our confidence is absolutely in our Lord, Who is the Way and **the Truth** and the Life (John 14:6). Before we turn our attention to the passages mentioned; let us first consider the different aspects of salvation as far as their context and timing is concerned.

## Past, Present and Future Salvation

"Bishop Wescott, when accosted by a Salvation Army girl with the question: 'Sir are you saved?' replied jocosely, (comically) "Do you mean esothen [I was saved] or sozomai [I am being saved] or sothesomai [I shall be saved]?" (Geo. Rogers, Studies in Romans, pg.34).

Without getting too technical it will be helpful to view all three aspects of being saved mentioned above. They are all built on the foundation that has been laid, the evangel of God regarding the faithful suffering and dying of the Lord Jesus Christ and are confirmed by His resurrection from the dead. They are also all referred to throughout the scriptures, especially in the apostle Paul's writings.

Although, the terms, "past salvation", "present salvation" and "future salvation" are not found in the scriptures, they are used to group together verses that refer to different aspects of our salvation. They are the packaging or the wrapping enfolding the truth. You may discard the wrapping if you must but don't deny the treasure inside.

## Our past salvation: We were saved!

When speaking of our past salvation we are referring to the fact that Christ died for the sins of the world almost 2000 years ago. God's work of redemption, through His Son Jesus was completed at Calvary. He was *given up because of our offenses, and roused because of our justifying* (Romans 4:25). It was then, He purchased us with His Own blood (Acts 20:28).

His spirit in us is *a pledge and foretaste of our inheritance, in anticipation of its full redemption—the inheritance which He has purchased* (Ephesians 1:14, Weymouth).

*Blessed be the God and Father of our Lord Jesus Christ, Who blesses us with every spiritual blessing among the celestials, in Christ, according as **He chooses us** in Him **before the disruption of the world*** (Ephesians1:3,4).

God had a complete plan  in choosing us long before we were born. His purpose for us includes our short time here on earth and continues after He snatches us away to be with Him.

*God is working all together for the good of those who are loving God, who are called according to **the purpose** that, whom **He foreknew, He designates** beforehand, also, to be conformed to the image of His Son, for Him to be Firstborn among many brethren. Whom He designates beforehand, these **He calls** also, and whom He calls, these He justifies also;  whom **He justifies**, these **He glorifies** also*  (Romans 8:28-30).

These achievements were accomplished wholly by Christ and are given to believers in grace. They are not out of us. In fact we had nothing to with Christ's work of redemption. These are God's gifts to us. **Nothing can ever overturn anything achieved in grace**.

Jesus is *the Lamb of God, Which is taking away the sin of the world* (John 1:29)! In God's mind and purpose, *the Lamb was slain from the disruption of the world* (Revelation 13:8, AV before the foundation of the world). God has no beginning and no end, therefore He does not dwell in time the same way we do. Before He created the eons or ages there was no day or night, no months or years; there was no such thing as time. In that realm or dimension He made His plans and established His purpose.

Christ was faithful to the end. He gave *Himself a ransom for all*, (1Timothy 2:6) and on the cross before He died He uttered these amazing words, announcing His absolute victory over sin, death and the Adversary, *"It is accomplished"* (John 19:30). That was the day Christ died for the sins of the world, therefore, since that day, **the sins of the world are died for!** These verses and many others reveal the absolute aspect of our past salvation. We had no choice in the matter and are literally **eternally indebted** to God and His grace, for so great a salvation.

## Our Future Salvation; we shall be saved!

As wonderful as our past salvation is and for that matter our present salvation also, we must conclude that the greatest benefit, arising from the cross of Christ, and God's saving grace, is still to come. Paul often refers to a further imminent and eminent salvation for the children of God:

*Being aware of the era, that it is already the hour for us to be roused out of sleep, for now is **our salvation nearer** than when we believe* (Romans 13:11).

Without taking anything away from the blessed intimacy that many dear saints have enjoyed, with the Lord, over the centuries, there is still a greater salvation ahead for them. Deep down we all long for a habitation greater than this old world. If our *expectation in Christ is in this life only, more forlorn than all men are we* (1Corinthians 15:19). Along with the entire creation, we the children of God are groaning in ourselves, aching to be freed from our mortal bodies.

*Creation itself, also, shall be freed from the slavery of corruption into the glorious freedom of the children of God. For we are aware, that the entire creation is groaning and travailing together until now. Yet not only so, but we ourselves also, who have the firstfruit of the spirit, we ourselves also, are groaning in ourselves, awaiting the sonship, the deliverance of our body* (Romans 8:21-23).

Therefore with patience we are *waiting for His Son out of the heavens, Whom He (God) rouses from among the dead, Jesus, our Rescuer out of the coming indignation* (1Thessalonians 1:10).

*For we are aware that, if our terrestrial tabernacle house should be demolished, we have a building of God, a house not made by hands, eonian, in the heavens. For in this also we are groaning, longing to be dressed in our habitation which is out of heaven, if so be that, being dressed also, we shall not be found naked. For we also, who are in the tabernacle, are groaning, being burdened, on which we are not wanting to be stripped, but to be dressed, that the mortal may be swallowed up by life* (2Corinthians 5:1-4).

We have a permanent homeland in the heavens. It has always been there. When the time comes for us to go home we will be given a new body suited to our celestial habitation.

*For our realm is inherent in the heavens, out of which we are awaiting a Saviour also, the Lord, Jesus Christ, Who will transfigure the body of our humilation, to conform it to the body of His glory, in accord with the operation which enables Him even to subject all to Himself* (Philippians 3:20,21).

The Lord knows all who are His, for He chose us; we did not choose Him (John 15:16)! Whether we are dead or alive, sleeping or watching, we are assured that when the trumpet sounds our **future salvation** is very near, even at the door.

*God did not appoint us to indignation, but to the procuring of salvation through our Lord Jesus Christ, Who died for our sakes, that, whether we may be watching or drowsing, we should be living at the same time together with Him* (1Thessalonians 5:9,10).

It is at this time we will be made alive **beyond the reach of death** and it is not until then that we will be **saved indeed**!

*Lo! a secret to you am I telling! We all, indeed, shall not be put to repose, yet we all shall be changed, In an instant, in the twinkle of an eye, at the last trump. For He will be trumpeting, and the dead will be roused incorruptible, and we shall be changed. For this corruptible must put on incorruption, and this mortal put on immortality. Now, whenever this corruptible should be putting on incorruption and this mortal should be putting on immortality, then shall come to pass the word which is written, Swallowed up was Death by Victory* (1Corinthians 15:51-54).

*The Lord Himself will be descending from heaven with a shout of command, with the voice of the Chief Messenger, and with the trumpet of God, and the dead in Christ shall be rising first, then the living who are surviving, shall at the same time be snatched away together with them in clouds, to meet the Lord in the air.*

*And thus shall we always be together with the Lord. Console one another with these words*(1Thessalonians 4:16-18).

I have a feeling we will also be shouting as we soar through the enemy's territory on our way to our celestial homeland. **Meditating on the evangel**, the suffering and dying of the Lord Jesus Christ, His entombment, resurrection and our happy expectation, will open the door to a **bountiful storeroom** of encouragement. We are not of this world and therefore often feel out of place, like strangers in a foreign land. By reminding ourselves that our time here is temporary and quickly passing by and that we have a **heavenly allotment**, a **permanent homeland,** can have a dynamic  impact on our outlook of life.

I am not suggesting that we merely develop a habit of "positive thinking" or visualizing good thoughts to make us feel better. If this were the case, it would only benefit the most disciplined, among us, those who can faithfully encourage themselves. What we are speaking of is much more than positive thinking. Our celestial homeland is a reality. It existed before the planet earth was created and it will continue long after this old earth decays and passes by (Psalm 102:26, Isaiah 51:6). By faith we can see it afar.

*If Christ has not been roused, vain is our faith - we are still in our sins!* (1Corinthians 15:17). But He has been roused and He has conquered death. He is *Sovereign, Firstborn from among the dead, that in all He may be becoming first* (Colossians 1:18).

"There is a tremendous reservoir of potential power in the realization that our Lord has been raised from the dead. Its implications are limitless. If He has accomplished this, He is able for all else. We have a Lord Whose power knows no limits, and does not even retreat before death, the last of all our enemies." (A. E. Knoch, Unsearchable Riches Magazine Vol. 104, pg.85)

Through believing the evangel, God's power for salvation, we, in spirit, enter into the reality of what lies ahead for us.

*On hearing the word of truth, the evangel of your salvation - in Whom on believing also, you are sealed with the holy spirit of promise (which is an earnest of the enjoyment of our allotment, to the deliverance of that which has been procured) for the laud of His glory!* (Ephesians 1: 13,14).

His spirit homing in us is the **spirit of promise**. It is the guarantee that the full payment of what was procured for us will come when we are glorified and finally at home. Console one another with these words. This is our **future** and **ultimate salvation.** How could it be anything less, for from that time forward we will enjoy life beyond the reach of sickness, pain or death and more importantly we will **ever be with the Lord.**

## Our Present Salvation

What about our present salvation, "**we are being saved**"? There are not only many confusing and contradicting teachings circulating regarding "getting saved"; there seems to be just as many that have to do with "staying saved". Although, they may be based on scripture they become untruths or half-truths if they are the result of misapplying verses to an aspect of salvation that was not intended. Relatively speaking, there is little about the scriptural facts, we have discussed so far, regarding our past and future salvation that is difficult to comprehend, if kept in their proper context. For the most part, they all announce or confirm the fact that, through Christ, we have been **saved from sin**, the curse of sin and its penalty. We just need to accept them as such and believe them.

However, when it comes to our **present salvation**, we need a more thorough realization of God's revelation, of the power of grace, in order to be saved from the reign of Sin daily, and from the *stratagems of the Adversary* (Ephesians 6:11). There is no doubt that Satan will take advantage of those who are ignorant of his devices (2Corinthians 2:11, Weymouth).

Not understanding the difference between being saved from sin and death and daily overcoming the flesh, the world, and the enemy, is the cause of much confusion. Rightly dividing the many passages and placing them in their proper context is excellent place to start. Once we grasp the grace in what Christ has accomplished, on our behalf, a long time ago, and what God has made ready for us in the future, then are we ready to, calmly and sanely, approach the topic of our present salvation.

We live in the present and life is often difficult. As members of the human race, we are not exempt from the doubts and fears, the pain and sorrow, common to all. In fact, because of our heavenly allotment, we are subjected to a "spiritual warfare" that non-believers are not. We are especially, 24 hours a day, 7 days a week, in need of God to either **get us out of trouble** or to **keep us from getting into more.**

We know better than to expect to be spared hardships but we long for endurance and patience with joy in the midst of life's afflictions. Our heart's desire is to be faithful to the Lord and to daily be *more than conquering through Him, Who loves us* (Romans 8:37). To whatever measure this is possible, it will be through the power of God for salvation, one day at a time.

Today is the only day we have; it is a gift from the Lord for us to endure, grow and enjoy. Today is our day of salvation and our time to learn to *get hold of life really* (1Timothy 6:19) and live it to the fullest. Not that we have any confidence in ourselves; it is

God Who makes us competent (Colossians 1:12). Our complete belief system, including our understanding of being saved daily, must be established on three basic facts. They are: **God's vast love** for us and His whole creation; **God's desire** and willingness to save us and all mankind; and **God's ability** to accomplish all His intention.

## The Paradox Concerning Salvation

Let us now return to the paradox we mentioned regarding "being saved", and consider the two passages we identified, that appear to contradict. They may well represent what, in my opinion, is the most common controversy in the scriptures.

*In grace, through faith, are you saved, and **this is not out of you**; it is God's approach present, not of works, lest anyone should be boasting* (Ephesians 2:8,9).

*I am making known to you, brethren, the evangel which I bring to you, which also you accepted, in which also you stand, through which also you are saved, **if** you are retaining what I said in bringing the evangel to you, outside and except you believe feignedly* (1Corinthians 15:1,2).

Identifying the Greek forms of the verb "to save", in these two texts will be most helpful. Greek verb forms have similarities to the English past, present and future verb tenses but are not exactly the same. In Ephesians 2:8 we read, "**in grace, through faith** *are you saved*". In this passage the verb saved is in what is called the "State" or complete verb form. "This form gives the state resulting from an action." (Concordant Literal New Testament, Explanatory Information, pg.609) This **completed saved state** is the direct result of the work or action accomplished through the cross of Christ. It states the absolute truth regarding circumstances, which now exist (Christ has died for the sins of the world) and refers directly to our past and future salvation. For example, when it comes to the **ultimate salvation of all mankind,** Christ's own, last words, before He died, sum it up beautifully, *It is accomplished* (John 19:30) or completed. However, the message, of the completed work of Christ, on the cross, is also God's power and the foundation, on which our present salvation is established.

In the other passage, regarding the evangel we accepted and through which we *are saved*, if we retain what is written in the evangel (1Corinthians 15:2), the form of the verb, "to save", is different. Saved here is in the "Act" verb form. It is the **incomplete form** with the action, of being saved, incomplete and still **on going**. (CLNT, Explanatory Information, pg.609) Because we have accepted Paul's evangel, as being God's truth for today, we are able to stand in it. And we will daily continue to be saved, from the devises and tricks of the Adversary by retaining the truths that are in accord with the evangel and by simply keeping our course.

Both positions represented by the two forms of the verb "to save" are true under different circumstances. One is **complete, absolute**, and **independent**, which **we had nothing to do with**. The other is a **relative** position that we are **actively involved** in.

Although, our present salvation is only possible because of the faithful suffering and dying of the Lord Jesus, it is still dependent on other ongoing actions. For the balance of this writing I will be referring to the process and operation of "daily being saved", unless otherwise noted.

## Dangerous Delusions

First let me address the saints who, not unlike myself for many years, have a vague understanding of grace and are enjoying a measure of freedom in believing the truth. Their natural inclination may be to abhor any message that smacks of religious bondage for fear of losing their freedom in Christ.

There is no doubt that there are those teaching a message today of legalism, as there was in the first century church. We are wise to avoid anyone that would enslave us and rob us of the *freedom, which we have in Christ Jesus* (Galatians 2:4). Paul states emphatically *"for freedom Christ frees us!"* None of us desire to be *enthralled again with the yoke of slavery* (Galatians 5:1). But on the other hand if we persist in living for the flesh, albeit ignorantly under the guise of grace we will become apathetic, indifferent or worse yet, a slave to our flesh, and miss out on the spiritual blessing the Lord has for us each day.

*For you were called for freedom, brethren, only use not the freedom for an incentive to the flesh, but through love be slaving for one another. For the entire law is fulfilled in one word, in this: "You shall love your associate as yourself* (Galatians 5:13,14).

Yes, we were chosen before the disruption of the world and designated beforehand to be conformed to the image of His Son. Yes, we were called and have been justified and nothing can jeopardize our future salvation. This is not the issue here; God has blessed us with a` freedom in Christ to serve others not ourselves. We do not want to discover, at the dais of Christ, that we **squandered our freedom** to fulfill the desires of our flesh.

*Each of us shall be giving account concerning himself to God* (Romans 14:12).

*Wherefore we are ambitious . . . to be well pleasing to Him. For all of us* [believers] *must be manifested in front of the dais of Christ,* (AV judgment seat) *that each should be requited* (recover, be repaid) *for that which he puts into practice through the body, whether good or bad. Being aware, then, of the fear of the Lord, we are persuading men* (2Corinthians 5:9-11).

Besides the fact that we must all give an account later; daily learning to glorify God in our body (1Corinthians 6:20) will have an enormous impact on our present walk with the Lord.

*Be not deceived, God is not to be sneered at, for whatsoever a man may be sowing, this shall he be reaping also, for he who is sowing for his own flesh, from the flesh shall be reaping corruption,* (decay, depravity) *yet he who is sowing for the spirit, from the spirit shall be reaping life eonian. Now we may not be despondent in ideal doing, for in due season we shall be reaping, if we faint not. Consequently, then, as we have occasion, let us work for the good of all, especially for the family of faith* (Galatians 6:7-10).

This is not legalism. This is not grievous; it is just good spiritual, common sense. If we persist in bad eating habits we eventually will have bad health. Living a self-centered life and seeking instant gratification will lead to depression and a host of other problems. The answer to fighting depression is not to further indulge one's flesh  but to help someone in need.

Paul wrote, *In all things I set an example, showing you that, by working as I do, you ought to help the weak, and to bear in mind the words of the Lord Jesus, how He Himself said, "It is more blessed to give than to receive"* (Acts 20:35).

He who learns the "secret of giving" at an early age is blessed his whole life through. This is also in accord with the good news of the grace of God, as we will see more clearly as we proceed.

Rest assured that the enemy has a counterfeit for all God's blessings. Serving and pleasing self looks like freedom but in the end reaps death not life. The evangel is a message that proclaims us **free from sin and self.** It has the power to produce in us the ambition to please Him and serve others. *If then the Son shall make you free, you will be free indeed* (John 8:36, Weymouth).

## A Fatal Fallacy

"A fatal fallacy is that salvation maintains itself by the mere fact of its existence. Justice, wisdom, and kindness do not triumph in themselves. They triumph because they are regnant in man and expressed through man in relations to others." (Frank Neil Pohorlak, Pauline Polarized Paradoxes)

Regnant means: dominant, superior in power, influence and importance. (Webster's Dictionary) Although our salvation was freely given to us, if it does not become  the all-important influence in our life, it will lay dormant accomplishing little. Referring to justice, wisdom, and kindness, he went on to say,

"They triumph in and through a man who believes himself to be related to God . . . Salvation can be sustained only by a continuing personal belief in the evangel, only by a personal continuing commitment to Christ Jesus as Lord, only by the translating of these principles into practices. Anything else is sheer mockery and a fraudulent and dangerous delusion. Salvation must be worked out, or be carried into effect, if it is not to decay and die."

In Paul's first letter to Timothy he entreated him time and again to continue in his commitment to Christ with words like this,

*Become a model for the believers, in word, in behavior, in love, in faith, in purity. **Neglect not** the gracious gift which is in you. **Attend to yourself** and to the teaching. **Be persisting** in them, for in doing this you will **save yourself** as well as those hearing you* (1Timothy 4:12-16).

He ended the letter like a father would pleading with his son,

*O Timothy, that which is committed to you, **guard*** (6:20).

In his second letter Paul writes reminders along the same lines.

*I am reminding you to be **rekindling** the gracious gift of God which is in you* (2Timothy 1:6).*The ideal thing committed to you, **guard through the holy spirit** which is making its home in us* (:14).


## The Dynamic Irony of Grace

There is obviously no room for apathy or fatalism in Mr. Pohorlak's view of daily salvation. In fact some may discount his summation on the grounds that it is legalism. However, we must note, he did not say, we must work to gain our salvation. Instead he spoke of **maintaining** what has been freely given to us in Christ. There is a huge difference in working to gain salvation and maintaining what we already have for God's glory.

The **absolute nature of grace** and the reality of our high standing **in Christ** is the basis on which we employ and enjoy our present salvation **in the Lord**. Walking and living in the joy of our salvation is more than just a mere **knowledge of grace.** *Knowledge puffs up; yet love builds up* (1Corinthians 8:1). *If we should be perceiving all secrets and all knowledge and if we should have all faith, yet have no love, we are nothing* (13:2).

A love for God and His truth is the key that opens the door into life abundant. In a mysterious but mighty way, **grasping God's grace**, through the evangel, **gives us power to avoid the very sins**, which human logic supposes will give us license, and cause us to eagerly commit. As ironic as it may seem, growing in the realization God's grace alone can fill our hearts with love, which in turn can deliver us from the bondage of Sin and enable us to fulfill the law, in spirit. **The entire law is fulfilled in one word**, in this: *You shall* **love** *your associate as yourself* (Galatians 5:14).

## Fulfilling the Just Requirement of the Law

*Nothing, is now condemnation to those in Christ Jesus. Not according to flesh are they walking, but according to spirit, for the spirit's law of life in Christ Jesus frees you from the law of sin and death. For what was impossible to the law, in which it was infirm through the flesh, did God, sending His own Son in the likeness of sin's flesh and concerning sin, He condemns sin in the flesh, that* **the just requirement of the law may be fulfilled in us, who are not walking in accord with flesh, but in accord with spirit** (Romans 8:1-4).

Although it was and still is impossible to be righteous in God's sight through keeping the law, God did not nullify the law by bringing the evangel of grace. The fact that some object to even suggesting that we can fulfill law, confirms how dangerous the doctrines are that blind God's people to truth. In a very relevant way God's people can and do fulfill the just requirement of the law by **walking in accord with spirit**; God's spirit of love.

*Owe no one anything, except to be loving one another, for he who is loving another* **has fulfilled law**. *For this: You shall not commit adultery, you shall not murder, you shall not steal, you shall not testify falsely, you shall not covet, and if there is any* *other precept, it is summed up in this saying, in this: "You shall love your associate as yourself." Love is not working evil to an associate. The complement, then, of law, is love*  (Romans 13:8-10).

Love is the complement of law and is that which overcomes the weakness of the flesh and fulfills all that law requires. The love of God that has been poured out in our hearts through the holy spirit (Romans 5:5) will do no harm to his neighbor.

*The fruit of the spirit is love, joy, peace, patience, kindness, goodness, faithfulness, meekness, self-control: against such things there is no law. Now those of Christ Jesus crucify the flesh together with its passions, and lusts. If we may be living in spirit,* **in spirit we may be observing the elements** *also*  (Galatians 5:22-25).

In the above passage are several bold statements, one right after  another. They are securely connected to each other.

1. Against the fruit of the spirit there is no law.

2.Those of Christ Jesus crucify the flesh together with its passions, and lusts.

3. If we live in spirit in spirit we may be observing the elements.

The elements is referring to the Mosaic system.
(Concordant Keyword, pg.87)

*God is spirit* (John 4:24). And *God is love* (1John 4:8). Love is the most powerful force in the universe. It is not a question of whether we are able to fulfill the law or not, but how do we? The short answer is this, "When we live in spirit, and walk in spirit, we bear the fruit of the spirit". In spirit we observe the elements of law because the fruit of the spirit far surpasses what the law demanded. There is a world of difference in meeting all the just requirements of law through *love, joy, peace, patience, kindness, goodness, faithfulness, meekness, self-control* and seeking to establish our own righteousness through keeping rules, rituals and regulations.

## The Spirit is Subject to the Law of God

*For the disposition of the flesh is death, yet the disposition of the spirit is life and peace, because **the disposition of the flesh** is enmity to God, for it **is not subject to the law of God**, for neither is it able. Now those who are in flesh are not able to please God* (Romans 8:6-8).

In contrast to the fact that the flesh is not subject to the law of God we know that **the spirit** that has made its home in us most assuredly **is indeed subject to the law of God**. Therefore, by walking in spirit we instinctively fulfill the law and eagerly attend to the teachings and persist in them. This is what brings us joy and peace and pleases our Father.

On the other hand it is impossible to please God or fulfill law in the flesh. Attempting to regulate or enforce rules and rituals has failed consistently in the past and will continue to fail in the future. Legalism and ritualism do not work. They cannot deliver the goods they promise and only bring death, but,

*If the spirit of Him Who rouses Jesus from among the dead is making its home in you, He Who rouses Christ Jesus from among the dead will also be **vivifying** (making alive) **your mortal bodies** because of His spirit making its home in you* (:11).

## Putting the Practices of the Body to Death

*Consequently, then, brethren, debtors are we, not to the flesh, to be living in accord with flesh, for if you are living in accord with flesh, you are about to be **dying**. Yet if, **in spirit, you are putting the practices of the body to death**, you will be **living*** (Romans 8:12,13).

Here our apostle is addressing his "brethren" in the Lord. His warning is this: if you continue to live for the flesh you are about to be dying. "We owe the flesh nothing, and it promises us nothing but death. But we do owe it to the spirit to put the practices of the body to death and thus enjoy the life which the spirit makes ours in Christ Jesus." (Concordant Commentary pg.238)

The spirit of God has made its home in us (2Corinthians 6:16). The riches of His glory are not only ours to enjoy after we are caught away to the celestials. The same spirit and power that roused Christ from the dead, dwelling in us, will bring vitality and life, and free us to put the practices of the body to death.

*Whoever are being led by God's spirit, these are sons of God. For you did not get slavery's spirit to fear again, but you got the spirit of sonship, in which we are crying, "Abba, Father!* (Romans 8:14,15).

We are given the highest honor possible; that of being called "sons of God". Of course there is pain and suffering in this life, even for sons, as there is for all mankind. Yet we know as His children, He deals with us as sons not as enemies or strangers. Further we realize these sufferings are temporary while our allotment from God that is eonian (age abiding).

*The spirit itself is testifying together with our spirit that we are children of God. Yet if children, enjoyers also of an allotment,*

50

*enjoyers, indeed, of an allotment from God, yet joint enjoyers of Christ's allotment, we know that **if we are suffering together,** that **we should be glorified together also** For I am reckoning that the sufferings of the current era do not deserve the glory about to be revealed for us* (:16-18).

We pray for endurance, patience with joy (Colossians 1:11) knowing that even our sufferings are from the hand of our loving Father, for our good. Besides, they can't be compared to the glory ahead for us. We could never suffer enough to deserve being **joint enjoyers of Christ's allotment**, the glory of which is far beyond anything we could ask for or comprehend.

## Everyone is suffering. We understand why.

*The premonition of the creation is awaiting the unveiling of the sons of God. For to vanity was the creation subjected, not voluntarily, but because of Him Who subjects it, in expectation that the creation itself, also, shall be freed from the slavery of corruption into the glorious freedom of the children of God. For we are aware that the entire creation is groaning and travailing together until now. Yet not only so, but we ourselves also, who have the firstfruit of the spirit, are **groaning in ourselves, awaiting** the sonship, the **deliverance** of our body* (Romans 19-23).

We are ironically caught between two worlds. We have tasted the glory to come but must serve our time here on earth. We are groaning to be delivered from mortality and yet don't know what to pray for,

*but the spirit itself is pleading for us. **He** Who is searching the hearts **is aware** what is the disposition of the spirit, in accord with God is it pleading for the saints* (:26, 27).

What we are aware of will suffice; that *God is working all together for the good of those who are loving God,* who are called according to His purpose (:28). If **God is for us**, it matters not who is against us. (:31) and **nothing can be separating us from the love of God** in Christ Jesus (:35). He is in control and He is leading us on, ever onward and ever upward. Let us take courage as we continue on.

# CHAPTER 3

## Carry Your Own Salvation

Let us now turn our attention to the passage Mr. Pohorlak referred to in his paper "A Fatal Fallacy". This passage regarding "working out our own salvation" is misunderstood by legalists and fatalists alike but holds truth worth pursuing.

Leading up to this passage is the entreaty, *let this disposition be in you, which is in Christ Jesus also* (Philippians 2:5). Christ Who was *inherently in the form of God **empties Himself**, taking the form of a **slave**, coming to be in the likeness of humanity. He **humbled Himself**, becoming **obedient unto death**, even the death of the cross* (:6-8).

Christ emptied Himself and humbled Himself. *Wherefore, also, God highly exalts Him* (:9). Christ's humble obedience preceded and was the basis for His exaltation. The same rule applies to us as well. The disposition of Christ in us is the basis on which we fulfill our purpose here on earth; that is to be prepared for our future allotment. Let us keep this in mind as we proceed.

First of all, "Work out your own salvation", the wording of the Authorized Version, in my opinion, is misleading. We will concentrate on the Concordant Literal rendering, which Mr. Pohorlak also quoted, starting with two verses.

*My beloved, according as you always obey, with fear and trembling, be carrying your own salvation into effect for it is God, Who is operating in us, to do His will, for the sake of His delight* (Philippians 2:12,13).

We can sense the tender compassions of God, in this entreaty by the term "my beloved". Christ Himself is often referred to as **God's Beloved** or Beloved Son (Matthew 3:17, 12:18, 17:5 and Ephesians 1:6). To be referred to as beloved is special. This is not a warning, or a threat this is an entreaty of love from the heart of our heavenly Father. To entreat is to console. The elements of the Greek word are literally "BESIDE CALL". (Concordant keyword, pg. 58) **The Lord is calling us to His side,** to carry our salvation into effect. The definition of carry is, to support while in motion, to carry on or bring forth. (Concordant keyword, pg.43)

It will be enlightening and edifying to consider the meaning of another word of significance. A deeper understanding of the word "obey" will shed much light on this entreaty and will be a focal point of this writing. The elements of the Greek for the word translated "obey", are UNDER-HEAR. It is to hear and heed. (Concordant keyword, pg.209) The prevailing idea is **attentive listening** or **paying close attention** and then **heeding**. This is how the entreaty begins; "As you always obey". A companion verse with a similar phrase is found in Romans.

*You were slaves of Sin, yet you **obey from the heart** the type of teaching to which we were given over* (Romans 6:17).

**Obeying from the heart** is the primary role we play in God's ongoing operation of salvation. This is where we must start. The entreaty is directed to those who, in the past, have always obeyed or listened to what they were taught. Now once again, Paul is exhorting them to open their hearts, and listen closely, even with fear and trembling, regarding making their present daily salvation effective. Let me suggest that "heart obedience" is one of the prevailing themes of the scriptures, from cover to cover. It is directly related to the overall purpose for us being here on earth as well as, to God's ultimate plan, for all.

## Listening and Obeying

Jesus told a parable and then followed with a question.

*A man had two children. And, coming to the first, he said, "Child, go today, work in my vineyard." Yet he, answering, said, "I do not want to." Yet subsequently, regretting it, he went forth. Now, coming to the second, he said similarly. Now he, answering, said, "I go, lord! and he went not forth." Which of the two does the will of the father?* (Matthew 21:28-31).

In today's language you could say, one moral of the story is, **talk is cheap**. There is little merit in the fact that the one son said he would go work because indeed he did not go. The other son, who had a "change of heart" and eventually went, even though he initially said "no", ended up doing the will of the father. By making this point, Jesus was exposing the sin of the religious leaders, who continually bragged how they understood the Law of Moses and the will of God better than anyone else. Their security was in the fact that they were the most educated in the scriptures and could tell others what to do. Two chapters later Jesus speaks boldly and gets to the heart of the matter.

*Therefore do and observe everything that they* (Scribes and Pharisees) *command you; but do not imitate their lives, for though they tell others what to do, they do not do it themselves* (Matthew 23:3, Weymouth).

The answer to Jesus' question, "which one did the will of his father?" is an easy one. Let me rephrase the question; which son listened to his father? Or what does a father mean when he says to his child, "**You didn't listen?**" He means "you didn't obey". Listening and obeying are synonymous. This fact takes on a special significance when considering the phrase "obeying from the heart". This is where real obedience not only begins but this is where it counts.

By their own admission, the Pharisees understood exactly what God required of them but didn't do it. To make it worse they pretended they were more righteous than all other men. Their inability to keep the law was meant to lead them to Christ, their Saviour. Instead they hated Him and crucified Him. Understanding what was required of them didn't benefit them. Little did they know that those who did not have the same understanding but were obediently living in accord with the light they had were much closer to the will of God.

## With Fear and Trembling

We will explore further the significance of obeying from the heart, as we continue. For now let us move on to the next phrase, *"with fear and trembling".* As we always listen, we are now to do the same, sincerely, even with fear and trembling .

Fear is defined as "an emotion excited by impending evil". (Concordant Keyword, pg. 105) God is the Creator of all, including evil (Isaiah 45:7). He uses good and evil to demonstrate His love and power, in the earth and sometimes to get our attention or to train us. He knows how to work all things for our good and bring lasting goodness out of temporary evil.

It is normal to get emotional about impending evil. Often we forget how much we are constantly in need of God's salvation until fear begins to grip our heart. In time of need we can not help but turn our attention to Him. *The fear of God is the beginning of knowledge* (Proverbs 1:7). It either causes us to run from God or run to Him. A heart close to God, one that understands His ways, will be drawn by his fear our awesome God knowing that His perfect love has the power to cast out all fear (1John 4:18).

We are the temple of the living God (1Corinthians 3:16). His spirit has made its home in us, taken His abode or permanent residence (1Corinthians 3:16, 2Corinthians 6:16). How lightly we so often take this fact. We do not deserve the great salvation we enjoy and it came at a very high cost, to the Father and to His Son, our Saviour.

When we get a glimpse of the sufferings Christ endured in procuring our salvation our hearts will be filled with thanksgiving and reverence. Two things should come to mind as we meditate on the unspeakable torture and pain He suffered. The first thing is that He did not deserve any of this hideous treatment. He was sinless and was **given up because of our offences** (Romans 4:25). We are the ones who deserve to be punished; we are the ones who offended God. He in contrast always did what pleased the Father (John 8:29).

A second fact that should come to mind when pointing a finger at the Jews, and the Roman soldiers who abused our Lord Jesus. It is this; "Except for the grace of God there go I". We may quote this phrase from time to time but do we dare admit that this could refer to those who committed the most wicked crime ever, the torture and the murder of the Son of God? Except for God's grace we also are capable of mocking our Lord, spitting in His face and even killing Him. This is a fearful and sobering thought, one that would cause us to fear and tremble if the full extent were realized.

Let us add up the facts. Except for God's grace we could be in the same class as His tormenters; though we didn't commit such crimes we deserve what Jesus suffered; instead of receiving what we deserve, we are chosen to be God's holy temple, His abiding place. A revelation of these truths will cause a soft heart to be broken and crushed. This is one sacrifice God desires and shall not despise (Psalm 51:17).

We cannot help but be filled with love and a reverent fear when we grasp the grace in our salvation. If we understand the fear of God we are able to glory in our knowledge of Him and all He has accomplished on our behalf. He gives us wisdom and comprehension. We don't acquire it on our own. He is our shield as we walk with integrity or honesty, and He guards our way (Proverbs 2:5-8). It is with this understanding of the term with **fear and trembling** that we will proceed to consider further this passage of carrying our salvation into effect.

## With Good Humor

To reinforce the fact that there is no dread, in a healthy fear of God, to a trusting, obedient heart, we will consider Paul's instruction to the slaves, of his day,

*Be obeying your masters according to the flesh with fear and trembling, in the singleness of your heart, as to Christ, not with eye-slavery, as man-pleasers, but as slaves of Christ, doing the will of God from the soul, with good humor slaving as to the Lord and not to men* (Ephesians 6:5-7).

At first glance it may seem strange to see these two terms, **"with fear and trembling"** and **"with good humor"** both in the same sentence, referring to the same entreaty. The entreaty is for slaves to be obeying their masters, as if they were slaving for the Lord. This is the kind of slavery that can be performed with good humor. A closer look at the term "slaving with good humor" will shed light on these seeming contrary verses.

One definition of the verb to humor is to comply with the mood of another, to act in agreement with the nature of or to adapt oneself to. (Webster's Dictionary) To have a fear or awe of God is to have a deep respect and reverence for Him. This healthy fear along with our realization of the grace of God in truth (Colossians 1:6) frees us to honor Him in the highest, from the core of our spiritual being. This is to obey from the heart.

When our heart cheerfully submits, our whole being naturally adapts and eagerly complies with God's mood, His spirit or tone. This inward reality causes us to concentrate our energies in true worship and devotion to Him. Love becomes our motivation, not a duty or obligation to outwardly perform good deeds. Obedience first and foremost takes place in our inner most being energized by *the love of God that has been poured into our hearts through the holy spirit, which is being given to us* (Romans 5:5). Walking in this realization brings a confidence and joy unspeakable. This is also walking in spirit, **slaving** for the Lord from the soul **with good humor**.

## Own Salvation be Effecting

A feature of the Concordant Literal Version is this; only the words directly carried over from the manuscripts are in boldface type. If we remove the lightface words from the text we are considering, the words added to make it more readable, we are left with the following, "with fear and trembling being own salvation effect" or **own salvation be effecting**. The verb to effect or to be effecting is in, what is called, the middle voice. English has two voices active and passive. Active is where the subject does the action himself. Passive is where the subject is being acted upon. Greek has three voices. In the middle voice the subject is affected, more or less, by the action. (Concordant Version, pg. 609)

I think there is some value in the illustration I heard years ago, to shed light on the middle voice. Picture an open umbrella appearing during a rainstorm. We did not provide the umbrella;

it was already there. If we were responsible to provide our own umbrella the verb would be in the active voice. The same would be true even if we had to open up the umbrella ourselves. On the other hand If God were holding an umbrella over us 24 / 7, so that we never had to fear getting wet, He would have used the verb in the passive voice. Somewhere between these two thoughts, we discover revelation truth, in the middle voice. The fact remains the umbrella is there and already open but we must step under it or we will get wet.

We encounter many storms in this life. Often we are to blame, sometimes others, but more often life just happens. Regardless of whose fault it is, or how dark the clouds may get, we need never fear losing our salvation. This is not the thought at all. Salvation is a gift, but we need to **carry the salvation we have been given, into effect**, with fear and trembling. If we don't take shelter under the umbrella God has graciously provided, we will surely get wet and quickly get cold and possibly suffer further ill effects; in extreme cases, even death.

Through the trials, temptations and struggles of everyday life, God has provided a way to be carrying our salvation into effect, one day at a time.

*You should not, then, be worrying about the morrow, for the morrow will be worrying of itself. Sufficient for the day is its own evil* (Matthew 6:34).

Today is the only day we have to carry the salvation, graciously given to us, into effect. The legalist thinks he is responsible to initiate the action and then work it all out. The fatalist passively sits back thinking God is doing it all. The truth is that although we are not in charge and not the first cause we are actively involved in the powerful operation God has set in motion in us.

## The First Cause

Connected to and immediately following the entreaty of Philippians 2:12, we discover a critical revelation, which is the basis on which we carry our salvation into effect; *for it is God, Who is operating in you to will as well as to work for the sake of His delight* (:13). The hinge-word "for" between these two verses is a causal conjunction introducing the logical reason. (Concordant keyword, pg. 114) **God is the First Cause of all.** Behind the scenes He is actively at work. His intention is steadily unfolding in the universe and in us, according to His delight.

God is operating all in accord with the counsel of His will (Ephesians 1:11).

He is working all together for our good (Romans 8:28).

He is operating in us to will as well as to work for the sake of His delight (Philippians 2:13).

In between the action of God, as the First Cause of all, and His operation of saving us daily is our part of submissive listening. Our listening or obeying from the heart is where we are actively involved. Our part is a secondary cause but a vital part in God's operation of carrying our present salvation into effect.

God's spirit is dwelling in us; the same spirit that raised Christ from the dead (Romans 8:11). The greatness of the power that was in Christ is operating in us (Ephesians 1:19, Colossians 1:29). To listen attentively, and to heed is in effect to submit or obey from the heart. Here at the core of our spiritual being we **do not let** not Sin reign in our mortal body (Romans 6:12). Instead we,

Let the peace of Christ arbitrate in our heart(Colossians 3:15).

Let the word of Christ make its home in us richly (:16).

Let the disposition of Christ Jesus be in us (Philippians 2:5).

When the spirit puts its finger on sin in our heart, we pay close attention. We do not want to give place to the Adversary (Ephesians 4:27) or cause sorrow to (AV grieve) the holy spirit of God (:30). We listen attentively to what the spirit is saying and repent, or change our mind, if need be. If we have harmed or offended a brother or sister we are compelled to speak the truth to them and put off the false, before the day is out, if possible, for we are members of one another (:25,26).

Our own salvation is being carried into effect "for", or because it is the **logical result of listening**, based on the fact that it is God operating in us. It is on the basis of God's operation in a submissive heart, to work His will and delight, that we are made competent to walk worthily, bear fruit and be pleasing to Him. Our confidence is in His operation of grace at work in us. Therefore, we *are glorying in Christ Jesus and have no confidence in our flesh* (Philippians 3:3). Paul's revelation and testimony was,

*In the grace of God I am what I am, and His grace, which is in me, did not come to be for naught, but more exceedingly than all of them toil I - yet not I, but the grace of God which is with me* (1Corinthians 15:10).

Paul credited the grace of God for all he accomplished. He goes so far as to say it was the grace of God in him doing the work. Yet, on the other hand, he exhorts us also,

*Not to receive the grace of God for naught* (2Corinthians 6:1).

Is it possible, to be the recipient of the grace of God, and at the end of our life, have little of lasting value, to show for it ? If not, what would be the purpose of exhorting against receiving the grace of God for naught?

## All be Doing without Murmuring and Reasoning

Let us move on to the next few verses of this passage,

*All be doing without murmurings and reasonings, that you may become blameless and artless, children of God, flawless . . .* (Philippians 2:14).

Again, the hinge-word, "that" separating the first two thoughts is so important. We are told to **do all without murmuring** and reasoning; **"that" we may become blameless**. Obviously, to never complain and never ask, "Why me Lord?" is the ideal. By the grace of God, may we continue to make progress, in this area. It will be helpful to realize that the verb "to become" is in the Greek Act form, which is the incomplete, ongoing form. Carrying our present salvation into effect and becoming blameless is a life-long process. On the other hand we must also understand that it is sheer presumption, on our part, to think we are blameless, while at the same time, murmuring against God. If that were the case, what is the need of the exhortation?

Speaking of God's judgments on the children of Israel in the wilderness, Paul wrote, *All this befalls them typically* and *was written for our admonition.* He went on to say that because they murmured they *perished by the exterminator.* I am not suggesting that we need to fear being struck dead but we do well to heed the admonition that follows, *so let him who is supposing he stands beware that he should not be falling* (1Corinthians 10:10-12).

The purpose of the entreaty is to remind us that we are not standing on our own. If we forget that **we are what we are by the grace of God,** it is then we are most likely to fall. And fall we will, in one area or another, from time to time. Our Lord is *able to sympathize with our infirmities*, for He also was *tried in* *all respects like us, apart from sin* (Hebrews 4:15). When we do fall, He is able to comfort us and deal graciously with us as a loving father. We can be assured there will be times we need to be disciplined by the Lord, also.

*What son is there whom the father is not disciplining? Now if you are without discipline, of which all have become partakers, consequently you are bastards and not sons.* (Hebrews 12:7,8).

*All discipline, for the present is not seeming to be a thing of joy, but of sorrow, yet subsequently it is rendering the peaceable fruit of righteousness to those exercised through it* (:11).

It is humbling to be disciplined, but this is how we learn obedience and not to complain or question God. Like it or not, this is part of the process of learning to do all without murmuring and reasoning; that we may become blameless and artless children of God, flawless.

## Appearing as Luminaries

*. . . in the midst of a generation crooked and perverse among whom you are appearing as luminaries in the world, having on the word of life* (Philippians 2:15, 16).

There is something gloriously unique about the children of God in contrast to this crooked generation. We stand out like bright lights in the darkness because we are adorned with the word of life. *In the beginning was the word . . . in it was life and the life was the light of men* (John 1:1,4). Without the living word in us, there will be no light. But if the word of life, the truth of the evangel of the grace of God, is the dominant force in us, the light cannot help but shine in us and through us.

"The 'word of life', or a *living expression* of the evangel consists in conduct so consistent with it that the life alone will proclaim the spirit of the message apart from its formal announcement." (Concordant Commentary pg. 298)

As we submit to the word of life in our hearts we become a living expression of the evangel. Possibly only our closest friends and family will see a difference, although this phrase *"appearing as luminaries in the world"*, may have further reaching implications than we can ever realize. Weymouth translates this phrase *"seen as heavenly lights in the world "* and The Dabhar Version reads like this, *"light-guardians in the cosmos"*. We may never know how far our light has shone. This is not our concern. Our part is to keep coming to the light of God's word, and let it expose and dissipate the darkness in us and then around us. The darker the day gets the brighter our light shall shine.

*Now, if our evangel is covered, also, it is covered in those who are perishing, in whom the god of this eon blinds the apprehensions of the unbelieving so that the illumination of the evangel of the glory of Christ, Who is the Image of the invisible God, does not irradiate them. For we are not heralding ourselves, but Christ Jesus the Lord, yet ourselves your slaves because of Jesus, for the God Who says that, out of darkness* **light shall be shining**, *is He Who shines in our hearts, with a view to the illumination of the knowledge of the glory of God in the face of Jesus Christ. Now we have this treasure in earthen vessels, that the transcendence of the power may be of God and not of us* (2Corinthians 4:3-7).

*Let your light shine before men, that they may see your good works, and may glorify your Father who is in the heavens* (Matthew 5:16, Young's Literal).

## Toiling for Naught

Paul closes his entreaty for us to carry our own salvation into effect with these words,

*for my glorying in the day of Christ, that I did not run for naught, neither that I toil for naught* (Philippians 2:16).

Let us wrap up this section with one more thought. In effect, Paul's conclusion is; if God's children who always obey, do the same, with this entreaty, to carry our own salvation into effect, with fear and trembling, and do all without murmurings and reasoning, we will become blameless and shine as luminaries in the world, having on the word of life. Also, if we listen and heed this entreaty, it will be for **his glorying in the day of Christ**.

The fact that we obey from the heart this teaching, which is in accord with the evangel will be the evidence that our apostle **did not run in vain**, or **toil for nothing.**

The flip side is, if God's people are not obedient to Paul's message there will be no glorying for him in the day of Christ, in that respect. He will have run the race before him for naught and his toil will be shown to be for naught. I do not believe this will be the case but he is making a valid point. Let us also, *beloved brethren become settled, unmovable, superabounding in the work of the Lord always, being aware that **our toil is not for naught in the Lord*** (1Corinthians 15:58).

*Now all am I doing because of the evangel, that I may be becoming a joint participant of it. Are you not aware that those racing in a stadium are, indeed, all racing, yet one is obtaining the prize? Thus be racing that you may be grasping it. Now every contender is controlling himself in all things; they, indeed, then, that they may be obtaining a corruptible wreath, yet we an incorruptible. Now then, thus am I racing, not as dubious, thus am I boxing, not as punching the air, but I am belaboring my body and leading it into slavery, lest somehow, when heralding to others, I myself may become disqualified* (1Corinthians 9:23-27).

The legalist is mistaken in interpreting this and other passages to mean that he continually has to work to stay saved. Paul is not talking about being disqualified from heaven, or anything due to grace. He is speaking about missing out on a prize or a wreath that will be given to those who race in a manner to be able to grasp the prize.

The pure grace fatalist is just as wrong, thinking it is all done for him and like everyone else he will get the same reward. Both see a part of the truth; let us run the race before us with endurance; toward the goal be pursuing *for the prize of God's calling above in Christ Jesus* (Philippians 3:14).

And *not be despondent in ideal doing, for in due season we shall be reaping, if we do not faint* (Galatians 6:9).

*Such is the confidence we have through Christ toward God (not that we are competent of ourselves, to reckon anything as of ourselves, but our competency is of God)* (2Corinthians 3:4,5).

## In Christ - In the Lord

*Endeavor to present yourself to God qualified, an unashamed worker, correctly cutting the word of truth* (2Timothy 2:15).

We have attempted to correctly cut (AV rightly dividing) the passages regarding the different aspects of our salvation. We have also considered our part and God's part in making our present salvation effective. There is merit also in noting the terms **"in Christ"** and **"in the Lord",** as they pertain to our salvation. These terms often represent two different positions not unlike the two contrary tendencies of God's people we discussed. Depending on which direction we lean, we will undoubtedly find ourselves attracted to one aspect and avoid the other.

In 1918, A. E. Knock wrote the following on this distinction.

"We wish to assure all, who are so kindly solicitous, that we have yielded not one inch of our high position in Christ. In fact, we, in common with some of our readers, have so emphasized our privileges in Him that it has, in some measure, diverted us from the full realization of our deportment *in the Lord.* Our duty down here cannot be adduced by a process of reasoning from our exalted station above. . . . It is of principal importance that we distinguish between our position *"in Christ"* and our obedience *"in the Lord."* These are distinct in sphere, one in heaven and the other on earth. One is for our faith; it is what we believe; the other is for our feet; it is what we do. One enlightens our hearts; the other illumines our walk." (Unsearchable Riches, Vol. 9, pg.4)

Frank Pohorlak in Vol. 63, pg. 87 of the same magazine wrote, "We are declared to be sons by the act of faith: this is our standing in Christ. We are required to become sons by acts of faith: this is our state in the Lord. We are declared to be what we are required to become. We are to become in act what we are in fact. The work of sonship is finished, the product itself unfinished."

These two distinct terms appear often in the scriptures; their applications may overlap at times. Also, other titles could be considered such as "Lord Jesus Christ". However, a few uses of "in Christ" and "in the Lord" will suffice to confirm our point.

## In The Lord

Paul called himself **a prisoner,** *in the Lord* (Ephesians 4:1). He said, "children **obey** your parents, *in the Lord"* (Ephesians 6:1). To the ecclesia at Corinth he asked this question, "Are you not **my work** *in the Lord*?" He answers his own question with "you are my seal of **apostleship** in the Lord" (1Corinthians 9:1,2). For the sake of **the work** *of the Lord,* Epaphroditus was near death, risking his soul (Philippians 2:30). We are in the process of **growing** into a holy temple *in the Lord* (Ephesians 2:21). Notice also, the ongoing actions in the Lord, in the following passage.

*My brethren, beloved and longed for, my joy and wreath, be* **standing firm** *thus in the Lord, my beloved. I am entreating Euodia and I am entreating Syntyche, to be* **mutually disposed** *in the Lord. Yes, I am asking you also, genuine yokefellow, be* **aiding** *them, these women who* **compete together** *with me in the evangel, with Clement also, and the rest of my fellow workers whose names are in the scroll of life. Be* **rejoicing** *in the Lord always!* (Philippians 4:1-4).

This entreaty applies to our present growth and salvation. We are to **stand firm** and be **mutually disposed** in the Lord. We are to **aid** those who **compete together** and to **rejoice** in the Lord always! Similarly the Ephesians ecclesia was exhorted to be **walking** as children of light (for the fruit of the light is in all goodness and righteousness and truth); and to be **testing** what is well pleasing *to the Lord* (5:8-10). Also apostleship, work, growth, and being a slave or a prisoner, are referred to as being *in the Lord.* It is not difficult to see that in the Lord we are to continue growing, working, obeying, walking, standing, aiding, competing and testing. These are ongoing, incomplete actions.

## In Christ

In contrast to the relative truth, regarding our ongoing service and the necessity to daily grow in the Lord, we are assured that our high calling and our position in Christ are absolute and steadfast, reserved in the heavens for us.

*God blesses us with every spiritual blessing among the celestials, in Christ, according as He chooses us in Him before the disruption of the world, we to be holy and flawless in His sight, in love designating us beforehand for the place of a son for Him **through Christ Jesus;** in accord with the delight of His will, for the laud of the glory of His grace, which graces us in the Beloved: in Whom we are having the deliverance through His blood, the forgiveness of offenses in accord with the riches of His grace* (Ephesians 1:3-7).

We are blessed with **every spiritual blessing** among the celestials, and we were **chosen in Him** a long time ago. We now enjoy **deliverance** and **forgiveness** of our offences. In Christ we are **flawless** in God's sight. All these blessings are in accord with the riches of His grace, which means they are freely given to us for the laud of **the glory of His grace,** which He lavishes on us. They are not dependent on our walk in the Lord. However, comprehending what we have and what we are in Christ gives us great consolation and confidence to walk in His love. Knowing that our lot was cast in Christ before we were born, and is secure, is a key factor in growing in the realization of God's grace daily.

*As Sin reigns in death, thus Grace also should be reigning through righteousness, for life eonian, through Jesus Christ, our Lord* (Romans 5:21). Some day the reign of Grace will be absolute and universal. For now, we are the first fruits privileged to let God's saving grace be king in our heart.

*Thus, the saving grace of God is training us to disown irreverence and worldly desires, that we should be living sanely and justly and devoutly in the current eon, anticipating that happy expectation, even the advent of the glory of the great God and our Saviour Jesus Christ, Who gives Himself for us, that He should be redeeming us from all lawlessness and be cleansing for Himself a people to be about Him, zealous for ideal acts. Speak of these things and entreat and expose with every injunction. Let no one slight you* (Titus 2:11-15).

Grace is our present day trainer. It trains us to be saved daily from the stratagems of the enemy so we can enjoy our short time here on earth sanely, justly and devoutly. This present life is often referred to as "boot camp". We need grace to train us to *suffer evil as an ideal soldier of Christ Jesus* (2Timothy 2:3) and to prepare us for our heavenly allotment in the next eon.

# CHAPTER 4

## The God Who Promises

### To Everyone Who is Believing

*What is the scripture saying? Now "Abraham believes God, and it is reckoned to him for righteousness." Now to the worker, the wage is not reckoned as a favor, but as a debt. To him who is not working, yet is believing on Him Who is justifying the irreverent, his faith is reckoned for righteousness* (Romans 4:3-5).

The Protestant Reformation of the sixteenth century was primarily built on the revelation that **salvation is by faith alone** and not by works. God used Martin Luther and the other Reformers to recapture this truth that seemed to have been lost for centuries. As a whole Christianity today still agrees in theory, or in word, with this truth. However, each organization feels the need to go beyond what is written (1Corinthians 4:6) and adds to God's word their own, slightly different set of creeds. Confession of belief in these doctrines qualifies one for membership in that particular church organization and is often considered the sign that one is indeed saved.

We established in the first chapter that our faith, itself is not a saviour but is the vehicle that transports us into the realm of grace where we are saved. By faith our eyes are opened to perceive what has been freely given to us (1Corinthians 2:12).

Our faith is a gift from God. *For to you it is graciously granted, for Christ's sake . . . to be believing on Him* (Philippians 1:29)

It is really the faith of Christ Jesus that procured salvation for us.

*Having perceived that a man is not being **justified** by works of law, except alone **through the faith of Christ Jesus**, we also believe in Christ Jesus that we may **be justified by the faith of Christ*** (Galatians 2:16).

The life, *which I am now living in flesh, I am living in **faith that is of the Son of God***, *Who loves me, and gives Himself up for me* (Galatians.2:20).

"The flesh, which hampered the law, rendering it weak and ineffective, has been conquered by the power of Christ, and has been made the organ of the Spirit. The force that subdues and mortifies the flesh is 'the faith of Christ'. He is the author and finisher of faith (Hebrews 12:2). He lived and wrought on the principle of faith. And His faith, triumphing over death, became the saving principle for man. Our faith, centred on His victory, appropriates the virtue of His faith. Faith is the link between the saviour and the sinner. The gospel is the power of God unto salvation 'out of faith and into faith' (Romans 1:16) – out of the faith of Christ into the faith of the believer. His faith is the source of Divine power; our faith is the recipient of it. His faith is the pattern of our faith. He is the author and the finisher of faith; we are His imitators."    (V. Gelesnoff, Paul's Epistle to the Galatians, pg.58)

*Not ashamed am I of the evangel, for it is God's power for salvation **to everyone who is believing*** (Romans 1:16).

The evangel is God's power for salvation to those who believe it. The opposite is also true; the evangel is not a source of God's power to those who do not believe it. The many entreaties also that are in accord with the evangel are only for those who actually believe them. By faith are they, *beneficial for teaching, for exposure, for correction, for discipline in righteousness, that the man of God may be equipped, fitted out for every good act* (2Timothy 3:16,17).

The entreaties will not benefit those who do not believe that they are for us, or that it is impossible to obey them. They will have little effect on us if we perceive them strictly as a doctrine regarding of our position in Christ.

Also, if we have not been given the faith to take these declarations to heart for our correction and discipline, it seems unlikely that we will be fitted out for every good act. Not only is our justification realized by faith through our Lord, Jesus Christ; but through Him we also have the **access, by faith, into this grace** in which we stand (Romans 5:1,2). Although, faith is not a saviour, yet apart from faith there is no access into the grace in which we stand and are saved.

In the evangel, *God's righteousness is being revealed*, out of Christ's faith for our faith, according as it is written: "*Now the just one by faith shall be living*" (Romans 1:17). **The righteousness of God is** through Jesus Christ's faith for all but **only** as they believe the evangel. We cannot earn or initiate faith by our own volition; it is graciously granted to us to believe. However, it is through faith we have access into grace.

Many have ears to hear and have heard the evangel and may even give mental assent to grace but,

*The word heard does not benefit those hearers, not having been blended together with faith* (Hebrews 4:2).

**Apart from faith,** it is not only **impossible to please God** (Hebrews 11:6) it is also impossible to have access into grace.

*A righteousness of God (is manifest) through Jesus Christ's faith,
for all, and **on all who are believing**, for there is no distinction,
for all sinned and are wanting of the glory of God. Being justified
gratuitously in His grace, through the deliverance which is in
Christ Jesus . . . toward the display of His righteousness in the
current era, for Him to be just and **a Justifier of the one who is
of the faith of Jesus**. Where, then, is boasting? It is debarred!
Through what law? Of works? No! But through faith's law. For
we are reckoning a man to be **justified by faith** apart from
works of law* (Romans 3:22-28).

We are **justified gratuitously in His grace** for a special reason:
To be **a display of God's righteousness**, not our own, in this
current era. God will be proven to be just, before all His critics
because He is the Justifier of all who are of the faith of Jesus.
There is no boasting for us because we were freely given the
**Jesus-like-faith**. Our faith, like our salvation and like our
righteousness are for the applause of the glory of God and His
grace (Ephesians 1:6,12,14, Philippians 1:11). This is the
message that is the power of God for salvation, to all who
believe it.

## The Pinnacle of all Revelation

The book of Ephesians, and particularly the first three chapters,
is often referred to as the highest revelation of truth for today.
This epistle takes us back before the disruption (AV foundation)
of the world, to the time when **God chose His sons**, in Christ
(1:4). It also takes us ahead in time to the oncoming eons, when
God will be *displaying the transcendent **riches of His grace** in
His kindness to us in Christ Jesus* (2:7). Here, also is the only
place in all of scripture where we find the term "**the purpose of
the eons**" or ages (3:11).

God has purposed to do a great work in His universe before time ends. Because the sons of God will play an integral role in this operation, He therefore wants to share with us the secret of what He has purposed to do.

*. . . In accord with the riches of His grace, which He lavishes on us; in all wisdom and prudence **making known to us the secret of His will** (in accord with His delight, which He purposed in Him) to have an administration of the complement of the eras, **to head up all in the Christ** - both that in the heavens and that on the earth* (Ephesians 1:7-10).

Before God started any of the creation process He had a definite purpose and plan settled in His mind, from beginning to the end. His objective, which cannot fail was to eventually **head up all in the Christ** both that in the heavens and that on the earth (:10). Weymouth puts it this way, "*the purpose which He has cherished in His own mind of restoring the whole creation to find its one Head in Christ; yes, things in Heaven and things on earth to find their one Head in Him*".

God knew, all along, that His creatures would wander away from Him, for a season. This time would serve as a training period to prepare them for His presence. His intention all along was to draw each and every one back to Himself with cords of love and then keep them near, forever.

The work of gathering all in, will be accomplished through the body of Christ, under the Headship of Christ. It is through the evangel of the untraceable riches of Christ that we are enlightened to see the secret of this impending, powerful operation. And it is through this life's experiences that grace is now training us and we are now being molded into a vessel of honour, to do our part, later.

*I (Paul) became the dispenser, in accord with the gratuity of the grace of God, which is granted to me in accord with His powerful operation. To me, less than the least of all saints, was granted this grace: to bring the evangel of the untraceable riches of Christ to the nations, and to enlighten all as to what is the administration of the secret, which has been concealed from the eons in God, Who creates all, that now may be made known to the sovereignties and the authorities among the celestials, **through the ecclesia**, the multifarious wisdom of God, in accord with the purpose of the eons, which He makes in Christ Jesus, our Lord (3:7-11).*

God is, even now, using His called out sons to make known His manifold wisdom, to the mighty celestial beings in preparation to gather them in also. We cannot even begin to entertain the significance of such a calling and our lofty expectation without a deep sense of awe.

*For to expectation were we saved. . . Now, if we are expecting what we are not observing, we are awaiting it with endurance* (Romans 8:24,25).

## Sealed with the Holy Spirit of Promise

*On hearing the word of truth, the evangel of your salvation - in Whom on believing also, you are **sealed with the holy spirit of promise** which is an earnest of the enjoyment of our allotment* (Ephesians 1:13,14).

The day we heard and believed the evangel is the day God took His abode in us. Our training began when we realized the grace of God in truth (Colossians 1:6). At that time we were **sealed** with the **holy spirit of promise.** This is the **Father's stamp of approval** and His pledge of security against any violation.

How can we be sure of God's seal and stamp of approval on us? The answer is found in the book of Romans.

*The spirit itself is testifying together with our spirit that we are children of God and enjoyers also of an allotment from God, joint enjoyers of Christ's allotment if so be that we are suffering together, that we should be glorified together also. For I am reckoning that the sufferings of the current era do not deserve the glory about to be revealed for us. For the premonition of the creation is awaiting the unveiling of the sons of God* (Romans 8:16-19).

The **spirit of promise** dwelling in our hearts assures us that we are His children and that we were chosen to be a part of Christ's allotment in reconciling the universe back to God. If we suffer together we will be glorified together, also. The word "if" is not meant to express doubt. Besides, we are sure all God's children suffer. Instead, it simply confirms the basis on which we will be glorified; it is because we have suffered.

God is steadily working all according to His original plan and purpose; every detail is unfolding exactly the way it was planned and precisely according to His schedule. Nothing is early and nothing is late.

*In Him in Whom our lot was cast also, being designated beforehand according to the purpose of the One Who is **operating all in accord with the counsel of His will**, that we should be for the laud of His glory, who are pre-expectant in the Christ* (Ephesians 1:11,12).

All He has purposed to do, will indeed be done. The whole creation is groaning in expectation, waiting for the sons of God to be revealed. God not only has **the desire** to accomplish His intention but He has also has **the wisdom** and **the ability** or power to fulfill all that He desires to do.

## The Complement of the One Completing the All in all

In Ephesians we also read that God *rouses us together* and *seats us together among the celestials, in Christ Jesus* (2:6); not literally, but figuratively in Him. These glorious truths had been previously  concealed in God (Ephesians 3:9) until they were made known to Paul by revelation, in accord with the secret of *the administration of the grace of God* (3:2,3).

What may be the most astonishing revelation in Ephesians, and possibly in all holy writ is this; we, Christ's body, are *the complement of the One completing the all in all* (1:23). Christ is the Head, and not only are we **complete in Him** (Colossians 2:10) but as His body we fill up or complete Him, also.

If these words were written in any other writing, other than  in the Sacred Scriptures, we could hardly even begin to entertain their validity or consider their meaning. Surely their full meaning will not be realized until we are changed and snatched away to be with Him in the celestials. For now, our spirits soar as we meditate on these things, even if our minds cannot fully grasp them. However, we have this confidence

*That He, Who undertakes a good work among us, will be performing it until the day of Jesus Christ* (Philippians 1:6).

The powerful operation that God has started in us; He will finish. As incredible as it may sound, we will be *completed for the entire complement of God* (Ephesians 3:19), for God has declared it and He is the One Who is able;

*able to do superexcessively above all that we are requesting or apprehending, **according to the power that is operating in us**, to Him be the glory in the ecclesia and in Christ Jesus for all the generations of the eon of the eons! Amen!* (:20,21).

God is in the process of working a work far beyond anything we could ask for or even mentally perceive, and as amazing as this may be, He is doing it in accord with the same spirit and **power that is now operating in us**. The expectation of what lies ahead for us can have a dynamic impact on our lives if we get a glimpse of it and meditate on it.

## With Men This is Impossible

Let me remind you that the Bible's chapter breaks are not in the original manuscripts; man inserted them, to make the reading of the scriptures user-friendlier. Therefore, the last verse of Ephesians chapter three is directly followed by and connected to the opening phrase, of chapter four, "I am entreating you, then". This is of special significance. This phrase and especially the word "then" connect the first three "doctrinal chapters" with the last three.

The whole thought Paul is conveying continues through the chapter break, without any pause, and is this: because of the glory prepared for us who are believing, culminating in the fact that we are chosen to be completed for the entire complement of God, and because God is able to do what He said He would do, even though it is far above anything we could ask for or even comprehend, **we are entreated then** or **therefore**, to walk worthily of this calling with which we were called (4:1).

It seems fitting, at this time, to borrow a phrase and share a passage referring to the salvation of national Israel. A young man approached Jesus, and asked Him, *Teacher, what good shall I be doing that I should be having life eonian* (life age-during, Young's, Matthew 19:16)? After a short discourse, Jesus ends His dialogue with the young man with these words, *If you are wanting to be perfect, go, sell your possessions and be giving to the poor* (:21). This was not what the young man wanted to hear and he went away sorrowful for he had many acquisitions (:22). Jesus, continued speaking to His followers,

*It is easier for a camel to be entering through the eye of a needle than for a rich man to be entering into the kingdom of God. . . the disciples were tremendously astonished, saying, Who, consequently, can be saved? . . . Jesus said to them, "With men this is impossible, yet with God all is possible"* (:24-26).

When it comes to our present salvation, we may be tempted to ask the same question, "**Who then can be saved**", especially if it depends on us faithfully retaining what Paul said, in bringing the evangel and then walking worthily of our almost unbelievable high calling? We must conclude that the answer is also the same, "**With men this is impossible**". How can we ever walk worthily of what we have just been speaking? And yet here we have the entreaty clearly stated in black and white.

Regardless of how we perceive what it all means to be chosen to be a member Christ's body and His complement, we must conclude it will be so and it will be glorious. No less amazing is the fact that we will be made competent to walk worthily of this calling. Both of these facts are above what we could ask for and more than we can at this time fully understand. Nevertheless, we are convinced that "**With God this also is possible**".

Even though we are weak mortals, often falling short of the ideal, missing the mark daily; with God, both are possible. We must not ignore the promises regarding our heavenly allotment or the entreaties to walk worthily because we don't see how either is possible. Like all scripture the promises and entreaties must be, especially *beneficial for teaching, for exposure, for correction, for discipline in righteousness*, that we may be equipped, **fitted out for every good act** (2Timothy 3:16,17).

If we find this whole matter too grand to be true, we do well at the very least to adopt the same attitude that Mary the mother of Jesus had. The message this young virgin received was no less difficult to believe. After God's mighty messenger, Gabriel told her what she was chosen for (Luke 1:26-33), her initial response was **"How shall this be**, since I know not a man?" (:34). After the babe was born three magi followed the star to the manger and a heavenly messenger also appeared to the shepherds who also sought out the babe. All these events must have been overwhelming for this young maiden. Listen to how she reacted, *"Mary was preserving all these things, pondering in her heart* (2:19). Weymouth says it this way, *"Mary treasured up all these things, often dwelling on them in her mind".* Shall we do anything less? In due time all will make sense. For now we believe, pondering His words, as we study further.

## Two Aspects of Truth

We have considered in depth 1Corinthians 15:2 and Philippians 2:12-16, regarding being saved daily, and how these passages appear to be contrary to the fact that we are saved in grace (Ephesians 2:7,8). There are many other verses that seem to outright contradict each other, also. As we eluded to in the first chapter, many deceived Christians blindly ignore or explain away numerous passages in order to cling to others are.

"The ability of the human mind to deceive itself is one of the major enigmas in man's checkered career, and not only able to but also desirous to. This is fact, not fancy. It is a fact that should frighten each one of us – that our love of the truth that we might be saved is not strong but a weak passion in most of us, and especially on this theme of salvation." (Frank Pohorlak, Pauline Polarized Paradoxes)

Many of Paul's **entreaties are paradoxes** expressing two aspects of the same truth. This may be one reason why there is so much controversy and deception regarding them. Listed below are a few examples taken from Mr. Poholak's study referred to above. We dare not discard either of these inspired truths or hold to one at the expense of the other. Instead we must accept them as God's declarations and seek to understand them by placing them in their proper context.

**With Christ have I been crucified** (Galatians 2:20). Later In the same epistle we read that *those of Christ Jesus crucify the flesh together with its passions, and lusts* (5:24). The first is a fact regarding our standing in Christ. The second is what we do, in the Lord, to daily enjoy our present salvation and to please God.

In Christ **we are a new creation** (2Corinthians 5:17). In the Lord, by faith we are to *put on* **the new humanity**, *which in accord with God,* **is being created** *in righteousness and benignity of the truth* (Ephesians 4:24).

*Whoever are baptized into Christ,* **put on Christ** (Galatians 3:27). However, in our daily walk we **put on the Lord Jesus Christ**, *and make no provision for the lusts of the flesh* (Romans 13:14).

We are the temple of God and His spirit has made its home in us (1Corinthians 3:16). Christ among us is our *expectation of glory* (Colossians 1:27), yet Paul travailed again for the Galatians for Christ to be formed in them (Galatians 4:19).

In his first letter to the ecclesia of God, which is in Corinth, Paul told the saints they were hallowed, **pronounced holy**, in Christ Jesus (1Corinthians 1:2). In his second letter he said *we should be cleansing ourselves, from every pollution of flesh and spirit,* **completing holiness** *in the fear of God* (2Corinthians 7:1).

Again in his first letter he said they were in Christ Jesus and He was their righteousness (1Corinthians 1:30). In the second letter we read, *the One* (Jesus Christ) *not knowing sin, He makes to be a sin offering for our sakes that we* **may be becoming** *God's righteousness, in Him* (2Corinthians 5:21).

In one breath Paul says, *you were once darkness, yet now you are light in the Lord* (Ephesians 5:8) and then in the next verse he says, *as children of light be walking* (:9) and in Romans 13:12 he instructs us to put on *the implements of light.*

It is one thing to hold dear the absolute truth that we died and our life is now *hid together with Christ in God* (Colossians 3:3). It is quite another to see the relative truth, that in the Lord, daily we are to deaden our members that are on the earth: *prostitution, uncleanness, passion, evil desire and greed, which is idolatry* (Colossians 3:5).

The legalist is blind to the fact that he figuratively died with Christ and in spirit his life is now hid with Christ in God. He still thinks he can control his members in the flesh by being more disciplined and resolves to try harder to be obedient to all God's precepts. In contrast to this the pure grace fatalist sees no need to deaden his members, his passions and lusts because his life is now hid together with Christ in God. Both hold to part of the truth and attempt to make it the whole. Again, our goal is to extract what is true and real from both positions and in accord with the evangel of the grace of God.

## Seeing From God's Perspective

*Abraham believed God, Who is vivifying the dead and* **calling what is not as if it were**, . . . *who, being beyond expectation, believes in expectation* (Romans 4:16-18).

In order to solve the enigma or the mystery surrounding the two aspects of these truths we must first comprehend who we are in Christ. If the eyes of our hearts have been enlightened (Ephesians 1:18), we are able to perceive the reality of God's perspective. The absolute truth of who we are in Christ is more than just a doctrine, it is the basis for who we are becoming, in the Lord, now. This is the life long process of growing in the realization of God, His grace and His will (Colossians 1:6,9,10). Jesus' advice to His followers applies to us, also.

*If ever you should be remaining in My word, you are truly My disciples, and you will know the truth, and **the truth will be making you free*** (John 8:31,32).

As we remain in the truth, faithfully walking in the light we have, more light will be given and more freedom enjoyed.

*You were called for freedom, brethren, only use not the freedom for an incentive to the flesh, but through love be slaving for one another* (Galatians 5:13).

Real freedom is not freedom to do whatever we want but freedom to cheerfully do what we know is pleasing to God.

*Being freed from Sin, you are enslaved to Righteousness* (Romans 6:18).

Truth is the key to open the door into freedom to grow in the realization of God. The more we begin to see the way He sees, the more we become like Him. God does not dwell in time the way we do. He can and does see us, as we will be when we put on immortality. He has determined the end from the beginning; both are as much a reality to Him as the other. He can call, what to us, is not yet a reality as if it were. The fact that He sees us this way, in Christ, gives us the faith to trust Him completely, knowing He will indeed accomplish it. In fact, it is already a done deal in His mind and purpose. Seeing what God sees, taking Him at His word, agreeing with Him and glorying in the security of His love and wisdom causes us to get hold of this truth and retain it. By faith, seeing ourselves the way God see us, gives us the power to walk in the spirit one day at a time. By meditating on His promise, it becomes a self-fulfilling prophecy in us, so to speak, and we gradually become, in the Lord, what God says we are in Christ.

The absolute truth of our position in Christ, and the relative truth about what we are becoming in the Lord, are not in conflict but actually compliment each other. We are to believe and retain what Paul said regarding both aspects of the truth of the evangel (1Corinthians 15:2). Faith in His declarations is a primary part of the process of becoming God's righteousness, in Him (2Corinthians 5:21) and a display of His righteousness in this current era (:26). We may be surprised to what extent our life here on earth is on display. God may not be the only one who sees us as we are in Christ. Paul said the apostles of his day became a **theater to the world** and to **messengers** and to men (1Corinthians 4:9).

## Objections and Perceived Contradictions

The most dangerous teachings are often not far from the truth but very near or part truths disguised as the whole truth. These teachings vary widely making it possible for millions to find a belief system and program they are comfortable with. For the most part Christendom doesn't seem to be aware of a believer's position in Christ. Many denominations all but ignore the apostle Paul's teachings on this subject. They appear content to occupy their time on the endless treadmill of rituals, ceremonies and meetings with a vague hope of the hereafter.

We will concentrate on the objections circulating amongst the ranks of those who do have knowledge of our position in Christ and rightly attribute it to what they call "pure grace". The purpose of the revelation of who we are in Christ is meant to spur us on, to be diligent, *not slothful, fervent in spirit, slaving for the Lord, rejoicing in expectation, enduring affliction, persevering in prayer, contributing to the needs of the saints* (Romans 12:11-13). Without a proper understanding of our walk in the Lord, knowledge of our standing in Christ will have the opposite effect. The purpose of grasping the grace in our calling and our salvation is to fill our hearts with love and motivate us to cheerfully slave for the Lord.

*For **the love of Christ is constraining us**, judging this, that, if One died for the sake of all, consequently all died. And He died for the sake of all that those who are living should by no means still be living to themselves, but to the One dying and being roused for their sakes* (2Corinthians 5:14, 15).

## Paul Never Reached Perfection

First, I must say this objection is based on the false premise that walking worthily and becoming blameless is equal to reaching perfection. We never intended to give that impression and hopefully by the end of this writing it will be apparent. In any event, Paul is our pattern and we are to imitate him according as he also did Christ (1Corinthians 11:1). He absolutely understood that he was **bought with a price** (1Corinthians 6:20) and his **life was not his own**. His advice to us is this,

*You fully follow me in my teaching, motive, purpose, faith, patience, love, endurance, persecutions and sufferings* (2Timothy 3:10,11).

87

The verses immediately preceding Paul's own admission that he never reached perfection (Philippians 3:12) reveal his love, motive and purpose in life.

*But, to be sure, I am also deeming all to be a forfeit because of the superiority of the knowledge of Christ Jesus, my Lord, because of Whom I **forfeited all**, and am deeming it to be refuse, that I should be gaining Christ, and may be found in Him, not having my righteousness, which is of law, but that which is through the faith of Christ, the righteousness which is from God for faith: to know Him, and the power of His resurrection, and the fellowship of His sufferings, conforming to His death,* (Philippians 3:8-10).

Following Paul in his sufferings is really partaking in the fellowship of Christ's sufferings and being conformed to His death. This is God's prescribed method to get to know Christ. Conforming to His death is almost a completely lost teaching amongst the saints today. Forfeiting all for Christ and being conformed to His death not only opens the door to knowing the power of His resurrection but also to grasping the concept of walking worthily of the Lord. A. E. Knoch wrote the following in reference to the Philippians passage above.

"Among the saints there are many, if not most, who cannot follow what is here set forth. They have many things in the flesh, race, position, attainments, and reputation, which they cannot forfeit for Christ. Of conformity to His death they know little or nothing, nor of the power of His resurrection. In a word, they are *immature.*"

Mr. Knoch went on to discuss the tendency among the saints to create an impassable gap between maturity and immaturity. He said, "The immature have no clear realization of their backwardness. They sometimes consider minority [being a minor] quite the normal state, and maturity an undue assumption. It seems a settled opinion that, in religion, there must be clouds and mystery. Clearness is only conceit. This comes largely because they are constantly occupied with the Scriptures intended for the immature."

He then explains how one can actually be a friend of Christ, while at the same time, also be an enemy of the cross of Christ. "Paradox though it seems, most of those who are friends of Christ are enemies of His cross (3:18). They are willing to part with their sins and evil and take Him as their Saviour, but they do not wish to part with their goodness or personal advantages and superiorities and be found alone in Him. They do not realize that the manner of Christ's death puts an end to all that man is in himself. They wish to be someone on their own account. And this makes them antagonistic to the cross." (Unsearchable Riches, Vol.104, pp. 88-90)

The issue is not whether we will ever reach perfection in the flesh or not. It is more about loving God with all our heart and forfeiting all to know Christ. Paul cheerfully submitted his soul, his life and his all to the Lord. This objection, that we can't reach perfection, is a given, and does not belong in our discussion; the enemy, threw it in to distract. The real issue is,

*So, if anyone is in Christ, there is a new creation: the primitive passed by. Lo! there has come new!* ( 2 Corinthians 5:17).

Along with our apostle may our testimony be,

*May it not be mine to be boasting, except in the cross of our Lord Jesus Christ, through which the world has been crucified to me, and I to the world. For in Christ Jesus neither circumcision nor uncircumcision is anything, but a new creation* (Galatians 6:14,15).

At the consummation God will be All in all, everything to everyone. At this time, He desires to be something special in us, the members of Christ's body. Forfeiting anything or everything to know Him will never be a disappointment. On the contrary, in Him all our heart's desires are realized. It is our logical divine service to *present our bodies a sacrifice, living, holy, well pleasing to God* (Romans 12:1). This is as natural as breathing when our heart is submitted to Christ. Through the power of God's evangel, in spirit, we can live for the One dying and being roused for our sakes (2Corinthians 5:15). The Father craves this response of love.

*Coming is the hour, and now is, when the true worshipers will be worshiping the Father in spirit and truth, for the Father also is seeking such to be worshiping Him. God is spirit, those who worshiping Him must worship in spirit and truth* (John 4:23,24).

## Justified Gratuitously in His Grace

To be justified is to be constituted righteous. (Concordant Keyword pg. 167) The gratuitous or complimentary aspect of justification will undoubtedly cause some in the "pure grace" camp to label this writing as being "under law". So afraid are they of losing their freedom to do whatever they please they desperately cling to the fact that they were,

*Justified gratuitously in His grace, through the deliverance which is in Christ Jesus* (Romans 3:24). And,

*By works of law shall no flesh at all be justified* (Galatians 2:16).

It is true, we are *constituted righteous* without any cause on our part. Although we do not merit justification, to conclude then, that it is impossible to walk worthily of the Lord is wrong. The scriptures do not equate being justified gratuitously in Christ as being synonymous with walking worthily, of the Lord.

This conclusion is based on a false premise. Our walk is on the earth, in the Lord, and our justification is our position in Christ. We have no desire to argue with the verses that confirm our justification is as free as the air we breathe.

The real argument, in scripture, is between, how we are justified; is it by the faith of Christ or by works of law? We readily identify the legalist's error in believing that being constituted righteous is the result of being good or the effect of obeying law. Under law a person can only become just if he obeys every commandment. If one is able to keep the whole law and yet stumble in one point he is guilty of all (James 2:10).

Saul of Tarsus, was a model Pharisee. He was well on his way to becoming blameless, according to the law, however he never quite made it. He well knew that, under law, strict obedience comes first and then one obtains a right standing, before God. Under grace it is just the opposite.

Through believing the evangel of the grace of God we come to understand that we are constituted righteous by the faith of Christ. As we grow in the realization of this truth, and walk in the light of it, we are changed by it. Under grace, the right standing in Christ, comes first, and then, walking accordingly in the Lord, follows.

Another aspect of the same false premise is this; *to obey from the heart the teachings we were given* (Romans 6:17), or to, *carry your own salvation into effect with fear and trembling* (Philippians 2:12) is equivalent to doing "works of law". Few would come right out and say that Paul's entreaties are not for us; instead they either ignore them or explain them away, or spiritualize the whole matter of walking worthily.

Walking worthily of the Lord is not claiming to be perfect. Neither is obeying from the heart, the teachings of the apostle Paul, mean one is seeking to be justified by works of law.

## Can We Do Whatever We Want?

Three scriptural statements are used to backup the delusion that we can do what ever we want; **Nothing is condemnation** to those in Christ Jesus (Romans 8:1), **All is allowed** (1Corinthians 6:12) and **we are not under law but under grace** (Galatians 5:18). These statements contain precious truth but not necessarily the whole truth. If taken out of context they become at best a part-truth and possibly gross error. They have been mistakenly elevated to the status of absolute truth for every believer in any circumstance. They have been repeatedly heralded, like a religious mantra, so much so, that many saints blindly accept them as such without question.

If we will honestly examine them in their context it will become apparent that they are indeed relative truths, subject to particular circumstances and further light. To take these verses as carte blanche for every situation would be like saying that justification is a pair of glasses that God puts on, so that we, His children, can give ourselves over to fleshly lusts and passions and yet all along appear to Him to be walking in spirit. If we carried this to the extreme, a man, "in Christ", could abuse his wife and appear to God as if tenderly loving her. This is a naïve and immature concept. There must be more to justification. Besides there are many scriptures contrary to this theory.

It is written, *the flesh is lusting against the spirit, yet the spirit against the flesh. Now these are opposing one another, lest you should be doing whatever you may want* (Galatians 5:17).

Paul does not conclude, because we are not under law, or because all is allowed us, or for any other reason, we can therefore do whatever we want. He says the opposite. The flesh and the spirit are opposing one another **lest we should be doing whatever we want**.

A few verses later he lists many works of the flesh and predicts,

*Those committing such things shall not be enjoying the allotment of the kingdom of God* (:21).

We find a second witness to the fact that the unjust shall not be enjoying the allotment of God's kingdom together with the very phrase used as the basis for the objection, "all is allowed me". If we examine the verses before and after this phrase in, 1Corinthians 6:9-12, it will shed light on the confusion. Immediately preceding, "all is allowed me", is the warning, *be not deceived* (:9) and then a list of the type of people who shall not be enjoying the allotment of God's kingdom. Included in the list are, thieves, the greedy, drunkards and revilers. He continues by saying *"some of you were these, but"*. But what? Are we still these? I think it would be silly, on our part, to come to that conclusion from the verse that follows, in which we actually have the word "but" three times; *some of you were these, but . . . but . . . but . . .*

**But** *you are bathed off,* **but** *you are hallowed,* **but** *you were justified in the name of our Lord Jesus Christ and by the spirit of our God* (:11).

Let us take a closer look at the two verses where Paul states, "All is allowed me", paying close attention again to the use of the word "but". The first one immediately follows the verse above and the other is found a few chapters later in the same letter to the Corinthians.

*All is allowed me, **but** not all is expedient. All is allowed me, **but** I will not be put under its authority by anything* (1Corinthians 6:12).

*All is allowed me, **but** not all is expedient. All is allowed me, **but** not all is edifying* (1Corinthians 10:23).

In all four cases following "all is allowed me" is the same word "but". The three statements, one repeated, are so simple a child can understand. All is allowed me BUT **all is not expedient**, all is allowed me BUT **I will not be put under its authority by anything**, all is allowed me, BUT **not all is edifying.** The issue is summarized in the closing verses of chapter 10.

*Whether you are eating or drinking, or anything you are doing, **do all for the glory of God.** And become not a stumbling block . . . to the ecclesia of God, according as I also am pleasing all in all things, not seeking my own expedience, but that of the many, that they may be saved* (1Corinthians 10:31-33).

It is clear that the determining factor in all our conduct is not to push the envelope as far as is allowed. It is not even to seek our own pleasure. Instead, it is to do all that we do for the glory of God and that which is expedient for the many we serve. The glorious irony in obeying this entreaty from the heart is that by doing so we find our true fulfillment and joy and are saved from many traps of the enemy.

Apparently, there are times when it is expedient to *answer a stupid man according to his folly, Lest he should become wise in his own eyes* (Proverbs 26:5). If so, then I do it now by saying, I suppose, for the child of God who is not concerned about doing what delights the heart of God and what is expedient and edifying to others, then I agree all is allowed him or her, in any circumstance, at any time. I speak as a fool!

Yes, all is allowed us in respect to the fact that we cannot out sin grace and even when we do there is no condemnation. Nevertheless it still remains that it is naive and harmful for us to put ourselves under the authority of anything that will jeopardize the enjoyment of God's kingdom, grieve the holy spirit or cause a brother to stumble.

As serious as this is, it is not the whole issue. We are not just speaking of enjoying our allotment now.

*For all of us must be manifested in front of the dais of Christ, that each should be requited for that which he puts into practice through the body, whether good or bad. Being aware, then, of the fear of the Lord, we are persuading men . . . We who are living should by no means still be living to ourselves, but to the One dying and being roused for our sakes* (2Corinthians 5:10,11,15).

It should be obvious that Paul was not advocating that we persuade men to do whatever they want because they are under grace, but the opposite. The context reveals that our persuading is in the form of a warning: **being aware of the fear of the Lord** is our motivation, realizing we are not to be living for ourselves but for Him and that we will be compensated accordingly, not only for good acts but for our bad practices.

## We are not Under Law but Under Grace

The fact, that we are not under law but under grace, may well be the underlying objection that the others ride on. This glorious truth can be so misleading. It has been abused and used in a manner that was never intended. Reading two short verses where the statement appears twice, reveals the purpose of this truth is not to give license to sin but the opposite.

*For Sin shall not be lording it over you, for you are not under law, but under grace. What then? Should we be sinning, seeing that we are not under law, but under grace? May it not be coming to that!* (Romans 6:14,15).

The powerful truth of being under grace is a key aspect of the evangel and a clearer understanding of it is a primary goal of this writing. **The evangel** of grace does not announce a freedom to indulge in sin but it **is the power that overcomes sin.**

Let us also go to the book of Galatians where we find a second witness to the fact that we are no longer under law. Once again, just by reading a few short verses where the statement is found will shed much light on the topic

*I am saying, Walk in spirit, and you should under no circumstances be consummating the lust of the flesh. The flesh is lusting against the spirit, yet the spirit against the flesh. Now these are opposing one another, lest you should be doing whatever you may want. Now, **if** you are led by spirit, you are not still under law* (Galatians 5:16-18).

The word "if" is an key part of the last statement *"if you are led by spirit, you are not still under law"*. It should be noted also that the verb to lead, or in this case, to be "led" is in the middle voice and also in the ACT verb form. We are absolutely involved in this incomplete and on-going action of being led by the spirit.

Both passages above state the fact, **"we are not under law"**. Let us consider the phrases connected to this truth. In Romans the thought is: we are not under law, *but under grace*; in Galatians it is, *if you are led by the spirit* you are not still under law. Let me suggest that there is a close tie to being **under grace** and being **led by spirit**. This is the reason they accompany the truth that we are not under law. Let us continue reading in Galatians where "being led by the spirit" is expounded on.

*The fruit of the spirit is love, joy, peace, patience, kindness, goodness, faithfulness, meekness, self-control:* **against such things there is no law**    (Galatians 5:22-23).

The reason is obvious why we are not under law if led by spirit; being led by the spirit involves bearing the fruit of the spirit against which there is no law. The next verse confirms this thought, *Now those of Christ Jesus crucify the flesh together with its passions, and lusts* (:24). Is it too much of a stretch to conclude that if we are not led by the spirit we will not bear the fruit of the spirit? And further, if we are not bearing the fruit of the spirit, then, we are not under grace but still under law?

Before we jump to any conclusions let us go back to Romans and read the verses that follow the declaration that *we are not under law, but under grace.* Hopefully they will confirm what it means to be under grace and not under law.

*Seeing that we are not under law, but under grace . . . . Are you not aware that to whom you are presenting yourselves as slaves for obedience, his slaves you are, whom you are obeying, whether of Sin for death, or of Obedience for righteousness? Now thanks be to God that you were slaves of Sin,* **yet you obey** *from the heart the type of teaching to which you were given over* (Romans 6:16, 17).

Presenting ourselves as slaves to Obedience is what exempts us from law. We were slaves of Sin but we **obeyed from the heart** the teaching regarding the evangel of the grace of God. It should go without saying, that those who are still presenting themselves as slaves of Sin are still under law, regardless of what revelation of grace they claim to have. Those who are led by the spirit are not under law. However, law still applies to the unjust, greedy, those who revile and wound with their words?

*Now we are aware that **the law is ideal** if ever anyone is using it lawfully, being aware of this, that law is not laid down for the just, **yet it is for the lawless** and insubordinate, the irreverent and sinners* (1Timothy1: 8,9).

The list of those who still need the law continues in the next two verses to include *paramours, sodomites, kidnapers, liars, perjurers and if **any other thing is opposing** sound teaching in accord with **the evangel** of the glory of the happy God, with which I* (Paul) *was entrusted* (:10,11).

In no shape or form do we advocate observing rituals, days, months and Sabbaths. We are complete in Christ; therefore circumcision and ceremonies will benefit nothing. It is not a question of whether we follow rules and regulations or whether we can do whatever we please. It is not either legalism or apathy. There is a third option.

*In Christ Jesus neither circumcision is availing anything, nor uncircumcision, but **faith, operating through love** . . . You were called for freedom, brethren, only use not the freedom for an incentive to the flesh, but through love be **slaving for one another**. For the entire law is fulfilled in one word, in this: "You shall love your associate as yourself. Now I am saying, Walk in spirit, and you should under no circumstances be consummating the lust of the flesh . . . Now, **if you are led by spirit, you are not still under law*** (Galatians 5:6-18).

Those not retaining what Paul said in bringing the evangel are not being led by the spirit and in experience are not under grace; their faith is feigned. They require law to know what is just. If we walk in the spirit of love our **actions far surpass the requirement of the law** for love will do no harm to his neighbor.

In spirit, we are marching to the beat of a much higher drum. As long as we live in our mortal bodies we will continue to fail or miss the mark daily but verse 16 says, *walk in spirit, and you should under no circumstances be consummating,* (completing) *the lust of the flesh.* We are not under law but under grace; grace will rescue us by filling our heart with faith and love.

## Nothing is now Condemnation

Let us look at one last objection and also consider its context: the fact that *"nothing is now condemnation to those in Christ Jesus".* The passage leading up to this statement from Romans 8:1, is Paul's long converse of Romans 7. If you have not read it lately, you might want to do so now. In this chapter Paul rehearses the futility of his past efforts in trying to become righteous by following law. He finds himself still in a state of wretchedness after spending years on the road, heading towards "becoming blameless". Instead of ever arriving he always fell short. Frustrated and condemned, he finally came to the revelation; the only thing that could rescue him from his wretchedness was grace. The chapter ends with these words.

*A wretched man am I! What will rescue me out of this body of death? Grace! I thank God, through Jesus Christ, our Lord. Consequently, then, I myself, with the mind, indeed, am slaving for God's law, yet with the flesh for Sin's law* (Romans 7:24,25).

Grace is the only solution to being set free from the tyranny of Sin that has plagued mankind since Adam ate the forbidden fruit. In this weakened state of mortality, the flesh helplessly slaves for Sin's law, as documented in Romans chapter 7. Immediately following this long preamble regarding mankind's curse, the rescuer is established. It is Grace. Let me remind you again there was no chapter breaks in the original manuscripts. Therefore the same thought continues into chapter 8.

*Consequently, then, I myself, with the mind, indeed, am slaving for God's law, yet with the flesh for Sin's law. Nothing, consequently, is now condemnation to those in Christ Jesus. Not according to flesh are they walking, but according to spirit* (Romans 7:25-8:1).

To quote half the thought is in effect to take it out of context. We must read it all to discover how grace rescues us from the wretchedness of Sin's slavery. How does grace succeed where law failed? The second part of verse one confirms the same answer as the Galatians passage did. Those in Christ Jesus, are freed from condemnation because not according to flesh are they walking, but according to spirit. So important is this truth that Paul actually repeats it again three verses later.

*The spirit's law of life in Christ Jesus frees us from the law of sin and death. For what was impossible to the law, in which it was infirm through the flesh, did God, sending His own Son in the likeness of sin's flesh and concerning sin, He condemns sin in the flesh, that the just requirement of the law may be fulfilled in us, who are not **walking** in accord with flesh, but **in accord with spirit*** (Romans 8:2-4).

The reason there is no condemnation, in Christ, is because the just requirement of the law is fulfilled in those who walk in accord with spirit. I have not found one verse stating the just requirement of the law is fulfilled in us simply by virtue of our high calling in Christ. Neither have I read one clear declaration of scripture that states, there is no condemnation for those who continue to walk according to the flesh. My experience has been the opposite and it has been painful.

It is misleading and harmful to conclude that anyone in Christ can do whatever they want, fulfilling the lusts and the passions of the flesh and assume there will be no condemnation. The spirit and the word must agree. Christ dwells in our hearts by faith (Ephesians 3:17) and our heart's desire is to please Him. To think that we can walk in spirit and fulfill the lusts of the flesh, at the same time, is an insult to common sense and a mockery to the clear declarations of Christ and His righteousness.

We have been set free from slaving for the lusts and passions of the flesh. All the flesh desires is fleeting and vanity. Our heart, the core of our spiritual being, will no longer allow us to be put under the authority of anything, except Jesus Christ, our Lord and Master, the One Who bought us with His own blood. As our realization of grace grows so does our desire to walk in spirit and we instinctively avoid that which is not expedient and that which does not edify. We willingly submit our heart to the teaching we have been given over to. Our hearts are now cheerful slaves to Obedience through the power of the evangel, in grace, through faith.

When God's word, by the spirit exposes our sin to us we cling to grace, which is greater than all our sin and therefore are free from condemnation. If we have harmed someone we humble ourselves and do all in our power to make it right. Like our Lord, we learn obedience from that which we suffer (Hebrews 5:8) and we go on daily growing in the realization of God.

*Not that I already obtained, or am already perfected. Yet I am pursuing, if I may be grasping also that for which I was grasped also by Christ Jesus. Brethren, not as yet am I reckoning myself to have grasped, yet one thing - forgetting, indeed, those things which are behind, yet stretching out to those in front - toward the goal am I pursuing for the prize of God's calling above in Christ Jesus. Whoever, then, are mature, may be disposed to this* (Philippians 3:12-15).

# CHAPTER 5

# Law Versus Grace

## The conflict Between Law and Grace

Let us proceed to explore what is the real conflict between law and grace. Any student who studies the whole Bible, sanely and calmly, can easily see that many exhortations by Paul are very similar to the precepts given to Israel long ago and also the teachings of Jesus, such as the sermon on the mount. Paul echoes the conclusion of the matter as Jesus gave; that the law itself can be summed up in loving God with your whole heart and your associate as yourself (Romans 13:9, Galatians 5:14).

Although no one can ever be justified by works of law, *law has become our escort to Christ, that we may be justified by faith* (Galatians 3:24). This was the purpose God had in mind all along and this is exactly what the power of God's grace is able to accomplish in us.

Where is the conflict then? Simply stated; what was **impossible for the law** to accomplish because of the infirmity of the flesh, **God did by sending His own Son**, *that the just requirement of the law may be fulfilled in us, who are not walking in accord with flesh, but in accord with spiri*t (Romans 8:3,4). The contrast is not between the objective of the law and the evangel of grace. Neither is there a contrast in how seriously one should take their particular calling and message.

For us, Christ's body, anyone called having been circumcised, it is common sense not to be de-circumcised. If anyone was called in uncircumcision, there is no advantage to circumcise.

*Circumcision is nothing, and uncircumcision is nothing but the keeping of the precepts of God. Each one in the calling in which he was called, in this let him remain* (1Corinthians 7:17-20).

God *will be paying each one in accord with his acts . . . There is no partiality with God, for whoever sinned without the law, without law also shall perish, and whoever sinned in law, through law will be judged. For not the listeners to law are just with God, but the doers of law shall be justified. For whenever they of the nations that have no law, by nature may be doing that which the law demands, these, having no law, are a law to themselves, who are displaying the action of the law written in their hearts, their conscience, also accusing or defending them* (Romans 2:6,11-15).

There is nothing wrong for the saints of God to familiarize themselves with the precepts of the law of God to better understand His hatred of sin, His high standard of righteousness and how the law dealt out justice. The error and deception is in thinking we can be justified in the flesh by keeping the precepts. Not that there is anything wrong with the precepts themselves. We are sure that *the law, indeed, is holy, and **the precept holy and just and good*** (Romans 7:12). The problem is in the weakness of the flesh to keep the law. The law was never meant to justify the sinner but to lead him to grace and a faith in Christ and His sacrifice.

*Now the law is not of faith . . . Christ reclaims us from the curse of the law, becoming a curse for our sakes. So that the law has become our escort to Christ, that we may be **justified by faith*** (Galatians 3:12-14).

*Now, at the coming of faith, we are no longer under an escort, for you are all sons of God, through faith in Christ Jesus. For whoever are baptized into Christ, put on Christ (:25-27).*

*For in Christ Jesus neither circumcision is availing anything, nor uncircumcision, but* **faith, operating through love** *(5:6).*

## Commandments are Promises

Under law, the so-called "Commandments", given to Israel were really promises that surely will be fulfilled in God's time and way. It will be helpful to consider the first and most important precept and the accompanying instructions.

*Hear, Israel! The Lord our God is One Lord. So you will love the Lord your God with all your heart and with all your soul and with all your might. These words, which I am instructing you today will come to be in your heart. Repeat them to your sons, and speak of them when you sit in your house, when you walk on the road, when you lie down and when you arise. Tie them for a sign on your hand, and they will come to be for the brow bands between your eyes; Write them on the jambs of your house and on your gates* (Deuteronomy 6:4-9).

Regardless how sincerely the children of Israel vowed to keep the precepts God had commanded, they just couldn't. Even in light of their many failures, there is an assurance that when God gives them *one heart*, and gives them a *new spirit* and turns their *heart of stone* into a *heart of flesh*, then will they *walk in His statutes* and *keep His judgments* (Ezekiel 11:19,20). God has promised that His **commandments** will come to be **in their heart** and then they will indeed do all that He commanded them to do.

Today, as a whole, Israel is blinded to the evangel. A *covering is remaining* over the eyes of their calloused heart. When God gives them one heart and a new spirit the covering will be removed but *only in Christ is it nullified* (2Corinthians 3:14,15).

What God has said, will surely come to pass when He once again begins to deal with Israel, His chosen people. They will be *a kingdom of priests and a holy nation* (Exodus 19:6). The apostle Peter confirms it also.

*You are a chosen race, a royal priesthood, a holy nation, a procured people, so that you will be recounting the virtues of Him Who calls you* (1Peter 2:9).

The writer of Hebrews adds some further insight,

*For this is the covenant which I shall be covenanting with the house of Israel after those days, the Lord is saying: "Imparting My laws to their comprehension, On their hearts, also, shall I be inscribing them, And I shall be to them for a God, And they shall be to Me for a people. And by no means should each be teaching his fellow citizen, And each his brother, saying, 'Know the Lord!' For all shall be acquainted with Me, From their little to their great* (Hebrews 8:10,11).

When this occurs, the greatest to the least will know their Messiah and they will love the Lord their God with their *whole heart, whole soul*, and their *whole comprehension* and they will love their associate as themselves (Matthew 22:37-39). It is then they will not *murder*, or *commit adultery*, or *steal*, or *covet* (Exodus 20:13-17).

## Similarities in Law and Paul's Exhortations

For the purpose of this study let us notice the striking similarities between Paul's entreaties and the instructions given to Israel to write the words on their door jams, to tie them on their hands and to repeat them day and night.

*Till I come, **give heed** to reading, to entreaty, to teaching . . . In these things meditate. **In these be**, that your progress may be apparent to all. Attend to yourself and to the teaching. Be **persisting in them**, for in doing this you will save yourself as well as those hearing you* (1Timothy 4:13-16).

Through the operation of the spirit in us we are naturally drawn to God's word, and specifically the instructions written to the body of Christ. Our heart cannot help but meditate on them and we instinctively persist in them. "**In these be**", is our joy and privilege. As we live in this reality, along with those also who hear us, we are saved from the stratagems of the enemy and from much of the sorrow of the world.

The above entreaty to Timothy is in accord with the exhortation that we examined earlier regarding our daily salvation!

*The evangel which I bring to you, which also you accepted, in which also you stand, through which also you are saved, **if you are retaining** what I said in bringing the evangel to you* (1Corinthians 15:2).

As His people and as the only temple of God on the earth today it is our honor to,

*Let the word of Christ be making its home in us richly, in all wisdom, teaching and admonishing ourselves; in psalms, in hymns, in spiritual songs, singing, with grace in our hearts to God* (Colossians 3:16).

As we station ourselves under grace daily and retain and persist in the word, living in it and letting it live in us we will be saved from the doubt, fear and unbelief that plagues so many of our generation. Our lives will become a living expression of the evangel and our progress will be apparent to all close to us.

We cannot save ourselves from sin or death but thanks be to our God, Christ has done it for us. We can, however save ourselves a lot of grief and be a blessing to others by putting on the armor of God and standing up to the Adversary. Let us not be ignorant of the things Satan apprehends knowing he will take advantage of us anyway he can (2Corinthians 2:11).

## Our Competency is of God

*Now such is the confidence we have through Christ toward God (not that we are competent of ourselves, to reckon anything as of ourselves, but our competency is of **God**), Who also **makes us competent** dispensers of a new covenant, not of the letter, but of the spirit, for the letter is killing, yet the spirit is vivifying* (2Corinthians 3:4-6).

The craving of our heart is for one thing alone, to know Him. Let us turn our full attention to this worthy pursuit and as we do, we will become competent dispensers, not of the letter of the law, but of the spirit. The evangel is spirit and life.

The evangel of grace has the power to overwhelm us daily with faith and love. Obeying from the heart, the teachings regarding this good news, is God's prescribed way to fulfill the just requirement of the law. When our heart submits, walking in spirit will follow. Presenting our bodies a sacrifice, living, holy, well pleasing to God will become our logical divine service (Romans 12:1).

As we walk in spirit, we *should under no circumstances be consummating the lusts of the flesh* (Galatians 5:16). The flesh and the spirit *are opposing one another* (:17). The good news is that our *old humanity was crucified together with Him, that the body of Sin may be nullified, for us by no means to be still slaving for Sin*, but instead reckoning ourselves *dead, indeed, to Sin, yet living to God in Christ Jesus, our Lord* (Romans 6:6,11).

*Now thanks be to God that you were slaves of Sin, yet you obey from the heart the type of teaching to which you were given over. Now, being freed from Sin, you are enslaved to Righteousness. As a man am I saying this, because of the infirmity of your flesh. For even as you present your members as slaves to Uncleanness and to Lawlessness for lawlessness, thus now present your members as slaves to Righteousness for holiness. For when you were slaves of Sin, you were free as to Righteousness. What fruit, then, had you then? - of which you are now ashamed, for, indeed, the consummation of those things is death. Yet, now, being freed from Sin, yet enslaved to God, you have your fruit for holiness. Now the consummation is life eonian* (Romans 6:17-22).

## Believing is Obeying

When considering, the revelations the glorified Christ gave through Paul, we must agree with Peter that some sayings are *hard to apprehend* (2Peter 3:16). Although, this is true, this is not always the case, Paul gave many clear declarations that a child can understand. It is these teachings that must form the basis of our belief system. We have to start with what is clear in order to gain an understanding of the deeper secrets. Why is it that Paul's writings in general and even the clear declarations of Christ through him are so readily ignored or discounted?

Simply stated, those who can't see don't want to obey.

"Men would understand; they do not care to obey. They try to understand where it is impossible they understand except by obeying." (George MacDonald)

So many appear to have a desire to understand the deep things of God but never come to the truth that only obedience, to what they already know, can open the door to more understanding. The root of the problem is not with the mind's ability to comprehend; it is a matter of submitting one's will and obeying from the heart the teachings we were given. This is a heart issue! The Scripture repays those who refuse it or misuse it with the inability to love the truth found therein. Paul clearly traces the reasons why people walk in the vanity of their mind and why they can't see the light of the truth and receive the life of God. He warns us not to do what they do and not to walk as they walk.

*By no means are you still to be walking according as those of the nations also are walking, in the vanity of their mind, their comprehension being darkened, being estranged from the life of God because of the ignorance that is in them, because of the callousness of their hearts* (Ephesians 4:17,18).

Let us place the sequence of these events in reverse order to see the progression. Firstly, a hard, **stubborn heart** brings the **ignorance** of a **darkened comprehension**, which causes an **estrangement** from the life of God. When a heart is too hard to accept and love new truth as it is being revealed, the **progressive decline begins**.

**Where will it end?** When Christ returns, the serious nature of the callousness of men's hearts, will be fully realized. Those who persisted on their stubborn course will be harshly dealt with.

*At the unveiling of the Lord Jesus from heaven with His powerful messengers, in flaming fire, dealing out vengeance to those who are **not acquainted with God** and those who are **not obeying the evangel** of our Lord Jesus Christ who shall incur the justice of eonian extermination from the face of the Lord, and from the glory of His strength whenever He may be coming to be glorified in His saints and to be marveled at in all who believe (seeing that our testimony to you was believed) in that day. For which we are always praying also concerning you, that our God should be counting you worthy of the calling, and should be fulfilling every delight of goodness and work of faith in power, so that the name of our Lord Jesus may be glorified in you, and you in Him, in accord with the grace of our God and the Lord Jesus Christ* (2Thessalonians 1:7-12).

When Christ returns, it is then that He will be visibly be glorified in us. Also at that time, those who do not know Him and those who did not obey His evangel will incur God's just judgment. A clear line is drawn between those who escape God's vengeance and those exterminated from the face of the Lord. A distinction is made, as the basis, for God's drastically different dealings with His people. Notice, those who believe escape God's vengeance. The others are exterminated from the face of the Lord, for **not obeying the evangel**. The analogy strongly infers that believing and obeying the evangel, are one and the same.

## Not I Toiling But The Grace of God in Me

In the book of Philippians we are provided the flip side to the downward spiral that occurs when truth is rejected and the evangel is not obeyed. This time it is a picture of the good work God began among us and will continue *performing until the day of Jesus Christ.* The passage is actually a prayer of Paul for all who stand for *the defense and confirmation of the evangel, the joint participants of grace* (Philippians 1:6,7). Paul realizing, this is a heart issue, begins his prayer, by getting right to the heart of the issue, which is love.

*I am praying, that your love may be superabounding still more and more in realization and all sensibility, for you to be testing what things are of consequence, that you may be sincere and no stumbling block for the day of Christ, filled with the fruit of righteousness that is through Jesus Christ for the glory and laud of God* (:9-11).

Love alone will bear fruit in the day of Christ. When love abounds for God, for His truth and for one another in a soft heart, a growing realization of things of consequence, such as God's grace and His will, is the result. This is followed by an ever increasing ability to sense and test such things, which in turn, creates in us a genuine sincerity. Instead of being a stumbling block for the day of Christ, God will be glorified in us and we will be filled with the fruit of righteousness that is through Jesus Christ. This is in accord with God's operation of grace from beginning to end.

*Yet, in the grace of God I am what I am, and His grace, which is in me, did not come to be for naught, but more exceedingly than all of them toil I - yet **not I**, but **the grace of God** which is with me* (1Corinthians 15:10).

As God's love is poured into our hearts by the spirit, *obeying from the heart,* the type of teaching to which we were given over (Romans 6:17) is not difficult or grievous. "To obey is to listen carefully so the message heard comes across to us and affects us. If God's word to us were a matter of law, our obedience would involve, first and foremost, paying careful attention to its instructions, and then carrying them out. But the word God gives is not a word of law; it is an evangel of grace, and grace is JOY. This message does not tell us what we are to do, but what God has done and shall do for us through Christ. Obedience to this message is a matter of earnest listening". (Dean Hough, Unsearchable Riches vol. 104, pg.33)

On the next page Dean continued with this, "We are to be declaring the evangel that Christ died for us while we are still sinners, and that we are identified with Him in His death, and shall be living to God as Christ is living to God, *not being ignorant* of such grace but be *believing it, perceiving it, taking it all into account and stationing* ourselves in mind and heart before God as He speaks to us of this word of gratuitous grace (Romans 6:1-13)."

Hearkening to the evangel is not, as some assume, submitting to the law. Attempting to obey law requires concentrating on self. Loving the truth of the evangel of God's grace and retaining it is a constant looking to God and what He has accomplished for us and even now is operating through us. The fact that we miss the mark daily is a given and although we don't take it lightly, it should not surprise us or discourage us, for long. God is working through our failures, which humble us and remind us of how helpless we are and dependent on His spirit and grace. A continual reminder of the weakness of our flesh and our unworthiness fills our hearts with thankfulness to God *for His indescribable gratuity* (2Corinthians 9:15)!

Also, by taking Paul's entreaties serious and by following the desire of our heart to please God we are not concluding that we can do any good on our own. On the contrary, we who long to live for the One Who gave His life for us, are ever mindful of our weakness and what was accomplished through the cross of Christ. To **love the truth, when it exposes us for what we are**, is possibly more, than at any other time, to obey from the heart.

## Be Walking in Them

We are convinced that every step of the process, including our perceived successes and failures, are all part of God's operation in us. **He is working all** together for our good. *He is the Former of light and Creator of darkness, Maker of good and Creator of evil* (Isaiah 45:7). It is an honor and privilege to be given this understanding and the faith to submit our hearts in anticipation of what He is doing. Immediately following the main text we began with, back in chapter one,

*In grace, through faith, are you saved, and this is not out of you; it is God's approach present, not of works, lest anyone should be boasting* (Ephesians 2:8,9).

We then read in the next verse following,

*For His achievement are we, being created in Christ Jesus for good works, which God makes ready beforehand, that we should be walking in them* (:10).

God has prepared good works beforehand for a good reason; that we should **walk in them**. By faith then, we walk, guarding *the ideal thing committed to us, through the holy spirit which is making its home in us* (2Timothy 1:14), enjoying our salvation and the comfort of *the love of God that has been poured into our hearts, by His spirit* (Romans 5:5). Our awareness of His love and our growing realization that we are called according to His purpose creates a deep desire in us to please Him. We can look forward to the good works that He has already prepared, glorying in the anticipation of them. Walking worthily is simply walking in the good works God has prepared for us beforehand.

Our hearts may have been broken many times but this is what has softened them and caused their roots to go deep and become grounded in His love. We cannot take credit for this work. In fact we would have chosen a much different path had we any choice in the matter and we will never forget the pain of what and where we once were.

*Once estranged and enemies in comprehension, by wicked acts, yet now He reconciles by His body of flesh, through His death, to present you holy and flawless and unimpeachable in His sight, since surely you are persisting in the faith, grounded and settled and are not being removed from the expectation of the evangel which you hear* (Colossians 1:21-23).

No longer enemies but being reconciled, we now enjoy peace with God through the death of His Son. We have been set apart and are flawless in His sight, since surely we are **persisting in the faith** and **not being removed from the expectation of the evangel**. Attempting to *live for God* while denying the truth of the evangel is merely to outwardly *have a form of devoutness, yet denying its power* (2Timothy 3:5).

## Where Sin Increases, Grace Superexceeds

One final truth that may be seen as an objection or at least a confusing issue is the fact that *where sin increases, grace superexceeds* (Romans 5:20). We have no argument with this fact! But how does grace far surpass sin?

The answer is not far to be found; it is given in the next verse,

*Even as Sin reigns in death, thus* **Grace also should be reigning through righteousness,** *for life eonian, through Jesus Christ, our Lord* (:21).

To reinforce this truth Paul asks this question in the verse following.

*What then, shall we declare? That we may be persisting in sin that grace should be increasing?* (6:1).

He answers his own question with *"May it not be coming to that!"* and asks another question, which warrants no answer,

*We, who died to sin, how shall we still be living in it?* (:2).

I have heard those who teach that we are dead to sin figuratively, while at the same time living in sin literally. Instead of pursuing this doctrine let me ask a question, Why would a child of God want to persist in sin? Grace does not reign through persisting in sin but through righteousness. The evangel, which is God's power for salvation, reveals God's righteousness *out of faith for faith*. Yes, righteousness is out of Christ's faith but it is for our faith. *Now the just one by faith shall be living* (Romans 1:16,17). We who believe we are dead to sin; how shall we continue to persist in sin. Like our father Abraham, as we **persist in believing** God's declarations, our faith is counted to us as righteousness (Romans 4:3).

## Grace Betrayed

"There is no power to compare with that of grace in breaking the shackles of sin. Yet, alas, how sad it is to hear of occasional cases, with only a superficial experience of grace, take advantage of their liberty to pervert it into licence to do evil! Is there any trespass so inexcusable as to make God's grace the handmaid of sin? God's saving grace has made its advent, and trains us to disown worldly desire, and *to live sanely and justly and devoutly.* Christ gave Himself for us, that He should be redeeming us from all lawlessness and be cleansing for Himself a people to be about Him, *zealous of ideal acts* (Titus 2:11-15)". (A. E. knoch, Unsearchable Riches, Volume 47, pp 55,56)

## Baptized into His Death

The first and most fundamental element of the evangel is the fact that *Christ died for our sakes,* (Romans 5:8) or *Christ died for our sins* (1Corinthians 15:3). The impact of this one act of obedience is mammoth and effects all mankind for all time.

One aspect of Christ's death particularly relevant to us is the companion fact that when Christ died we died with Him, not literally but in Him. In the following passage Paul says we are to reckon His death as ours and thereby our connection with sin also. By doing so, this in turn, allows us to walk in the same newness of life.

*Are you ignorant that whoever are baptized into Christ Jesus, are **baptized into His death**? We, then, were entombed together with Him through baptism into death, that, even as Christ was roused from among the dead through the glory of the Father, thus we also should be **walking in newness of life.** For if we have become planted together in the likeness of His death, nevertheless we shall be of the resurrection also, knowing this, that our old humanity was crucified together with Him, that the body of Sin may be nullified, for us by no means to be still slaving for Sin . . . Thus you also, **be reckoning yourselves to be dead, indeed, to Sin, yet living to God in Christ Jesus,** our Lord. **Let not Sin, then, be reigning in your mortal body,** for you to be obeying its lusts. Nor yet be presenting your members, as implements of injustice, to Sin, but present yourselves to God as if alive from among the dead, and your members as implements of righteousness to God. For **Sin shall not be lording it over you, for you are not under law, but under grace** (Romans 6:3-14).*

Being baptized into Christ's death and dying with Him is one of those teachings that may be difficult to understand, yet Paul wrote much about it. He said that the **old humanity** was

**crucified** together with Christ Jesus. This truth is connected to the evangel that empowers us to **no longer be slaving for Sin** as we **reckon ourselves dead to Sin** yet living to God in Christ.

We have His spirit and life abiding in us. This alone prevents Sin from reigning in our mortal body; we are no longer slaves to the lusts in our members but we are **free to present ourselves to God as if alive from the dead** and our members as tools of righteousness. Sin cannot lord it over us any longer because we are not under law but under grace. In light of this truth we are to daily present ourselves to God as if alive from the dead.

This is the way Jessie Penn-Lewis put it in her book "the Cross – the Touchstone of Faith", page 30.

"By faith you "reckon" that you died with Christ, and as you thus "reckon" the Holy Spirit applies that death to you, as you obey the ever-increasing light He throws on your life and actions. The "objective" and "subjective" must be kept in balance. Take Romans 6 as *absolute in experience* as well as in judicial position, without other Scriptures to interpret and supplement it, and you will be in danger of not calling sin – SIN; and you will close the door of your mind to the Holy Spirit's light upon deeper knowledge of yourself and God. You would be shut up to the simple maintaining of a "position," with no open vista of deeper experimental knowledge of Calvary, and what Galatians 2:20 means. "You have been crucified with Christ" . . . this includes the "self-life" as well as "sin." This will take the whole of the lifetime, and the work will not be completed *subjectively* until even the body of our humiliation is "conformed to the body of His glory" (Philippians 3:21), or in other words – the objective fact of "died with Christ" is complete, but the *subjective application* from center to circumference ends only with the final redemption of the body, when He shall come to be admired in all them that believe (2Thessalonians 1:10).

Galatians 2:20 is *the outcome of the faith position* of Romans 6. We "reckon" God's fact, and then declare "I have been crucified," whilst in detail we are day by day *made conformable* in experience, and obey Romans 6:13 in practice." (end of quote)

Closer to the end of this writing we will look at the practical aspects of being baptized into Christ's death and the meaning of "When He died we died". I will however, at this time, briefly consider a verse that sheds light on this truth.

*For let this disposition be in you, which is in Christ Jesus also* (Philippians 2:5).

There is a strong connection between being baptized into Christ's death and letting the disposition that is in Christ be in us, also. One's disposition is the result of one's inclinations. (Concordant keyword pg. 79) In other words, disposition is their character, temperament, makeup or personality.

Christ was *inherently in the form of God*, and *deems it not pillaging to be equal with God, nevertheless* His disposition was such that He *empties Himself, taking the form of a slave, coming to be in the likeness of humanity, and, being found in fashion as a human, He humbles Himself, becoming obedient unto death, even the death of the cross* (:6-8).

Christ humbled Himself and became obedient to death. He gave up His glory and all the rights He had previously enjoyed, and took the form of a slave. A slave has no rights; his whole purpose in life is to serve the master that owns him. Reckoning ourselves dead has to do with humbling ourselves also. As we do, God exalts us in a way that allows us to walk in newness of life. The verses preceding verse five give practical instruction as to the manner in which we are to be identified with His death.

*Fill my joy full, that you may be **mutually disposed**, having **mutual love**, joined in soul, being **disposed to one thing nothing** according **with faction**, **nor** yet according with **vainglory** - but with **humility**, deeming one another superior to one's self, not each noting that which is his own, but each that of others also* (:2-4). As mentioned we will discuss this in more detail later on.


## To Know Him

*It is eonian life that they may know Thee, the only true God, and Him Whom Thou dost commission, Jesus Christ* (John 17:3).

Some of us have spent countless hours and much energy studying, even debating these doctrines. At some point we must move on beyond doctrine if we are to really know Him intimately. Growing in the realization of God takes place by walking obediently, in the light we have been given, one day at a time, and one step at a time. There is only so much we can learn by studying, writing and talking; growing to maturity in the realization of the truth can come only through experience. It took some of us years and much pain to realize that we will never be constituted righteous by works of law. This was a necessary step of our journey to maturity and in realizing how we do fulfill the just requirement of the law.

*The law has become our escort to Christ, that we may be justified by faith. Now, at the coming of faith, we are no longer under an escort, for you are all sons of God, through faith in Christ Jesus. For whoever are baptized into Christ, put on Christ* (Galatians 3:24-27).

We are in Christ, and we are a new creation (2Corinthians 5:17). In Him we are complete (Colossians 2:10). Do we just sit back now and wait for our Lord to come for us? Paul wanted more! He wanted to **know Christ** and he wanted to **put on Christ**.

*But, to be sure, I am also deeming all to be a forfeit because of the superiority of the knowledge of Christ Jesus, my Lord, because of Whom I forfeited all, and am deeming it to be refuse, that I should be gaining Christ, and may be found in Him, not having my righteousness, which is of law, but that which is through the faith of Christ, the righteousness which is from God for faith* (Philippians 3:8,9).

Paul forfeited all to gain Christ and to be found in Him. Now he sets his sights on something even greater than this. Under law his goal was to live a perfect life. Now his goal is to know Christ in an intimate and powerful way.

*To know Him, and the power of His resurrection, and the fellowship of His sufferings, conforming to His death, if somehow I should be attaining to the resurrection that is out from among the dead. Not that I already obtained, or am already perfected. Yet I am **pursuing,** if I may be **grasping** also that for which I was grasped also by Christ Jesus. Brethren, not as yet am I reckoning myself to have grasped, yet one thing - forgetting, indeed, those things which are behind, yet **stretching out** to those in front - toward the goal am I **pursuing** for the prize of God's calling above in Christ Jesus* (10-14).

Our ultimate goal will not be realized until we are changed into the glorious image of Christ, Who is the Firstborn out from the dead. In the meantime we have the earnest of the spirit. In a very real way we are seated with Him in the celestials because His spirit has taken its abode in us. We cannot know Christ now, the way we will but as we commune with Him, and walk in spirit with Him we can enjoy the earnest of resurrection life, in our present experience, far beyond what any words can tell.

Paul admitted that he had not been perfected or obtained the life he longed for but he never stopped pursuing it, grasping for it. All his goals in life were dropped for this one pursuit. Both successes and failures of the past were forgotten and left behind in order to concentrate fully on stretching out to the goal for the prize of God's calling above in Christ Jesus. Unless we share this same passion, we have no idea what we are missing. There is a place in God, the saints can enjoy, beyond anything this world can offer but, how few care to forfeit all to have it. To the mature who have a craving for this reality Paul offers this appeal and advice.

*Whoever, then, are mature, may be disposed to this, and if in anything you are differently disposed, this also shall God reveal to you. Moreover, in what we outstrip others, there is to be a mutual disposition to be observing the elements by the same rule. Become imitators together of me* (:15-17).

We are not to concern ourselves with who has more zeal or faith than we do or who appears to be ahead of the others in the race. Instead our eyes are on Christ as we stay on course, persisting in the faith, striving for the same goal. When our days on earth near their end, may we have the same testimony and expectation as Paul, our apostle and our pattern.

*I have contended the ideal contest. I have finished my career. I have kept the faith Furthermore, there is reserved for me the wreath of righteousness, which the Lord, the just Judge, will be paying to me in that day; yet not to me only, but also to all who love His advent* (2Timothy 4:7,8).

## Transformed into His Image

"To know Christ is to be made like Him. It is in beholding the image that we are changed into it, transformed by what we love." (Elizabeth Elliot, The Liberty of Obedience)

Absolute truth has been established. God is *working all in accord with the counsel of His will* (Ephesians 1:11)! He is *working all together for our good* (Romans 8:28)! He is the First Cause of all! However, we are actively involved. Our response to what He has accomplished, and promised, and is still working in us, is to obey the evangel, from the heart.

*Stripping off the old humanity, together with its practices, and putting on the young, which is being **renewed into recognition;** to accord **with the Image** of the One Who creates it* (Colossians 3:9,10).

*Now we all, with uncovered face, mirroring the Lord's glory, are being **transformed into the same image**, from glory to glory, even as from the Lord, the spirit* (2Corinthians 3:18).

The word translated in English as "transform" comes from the Greek *meta morph o*, which is very similar to our English word metamorphosis. The transformation of a caterpillar into a butterfly is a fitting analogy of the process we are going through into the image of our Lord.

We cannot create our own beauty or light. As the moon simply reflects the light of the sun so we mirror the Lord's glory. Putting on the new humanity is the transformation by the spirit in us, from glory to glory.

*The path of the righteous is like the light of dawn's brightness, Advancing and becoming resplendent until the day is established* (Proverbs 4:18).

*Wherefore He is saying, 'Rouse! O drowsy one, and rise from among the dead, and **Christ shall dawn upon you**!' Be observing accurately, then, brethren, how you are walking, not as unwise, but as wise* (Ephesians 5:14,15).

*Contend the ideal contest of the faith. Get hold of eonian life, for which you were called* (1Timothy 6:12).

Contending the ideal contest is the only way to fulfill our heart's desire. This is in accord with walking worthily and is pleasing to our Lord. God's chosen and called will not find fulfillment in this life in any other pursuit, regardless how hard we try.


## Except Through Law, Sin is Not Known

As we previously mentioned, the precepts of the law, given to Israel, were not commandments that God expected His people to actually be able to fulfill at that time. As the Creator of all and the Knower of all, He is well aware of the weakness of the flesh. He had no delusions about His children's ability, or should we say, their inability to follow through with their pledge to obey all that He had commanded them, although they promised many times that they would.

In spite of Israel's failure to keep their end of the agreement, and in spite of God's foreknowledge of this fact, the precepts were given to them for good reason. Israel's experience with law served God's intended purpose and was written for our learning, also. The law clearly revealed God's standards of righteousness, His hatred of sin, and it also exposed man's total weakness through the flesh. Except through law, sin is not known (Romans 7:7). The law was given *that the sin might become exceeding sinful through the command* (:13, Young's Literal). When it comes to being righteous, all mankind, even His chosen race, is utterly helpless in himself and wholly dependent on grace. But the fact remains that God's hatred of sin and His standard of righteousness has not changed during this administration of the grace of God.

## Faith Sustains Law

The nation of Israel has been temporarily set aside during this administration. When God is done dealing with the nations he will once again deal with Israel in a mighty way and before He is done they will all be saved.

*For I am not willing for you to be ignorant of this secret, brethren, lest you may be passing for prudent among yourselves, that callousness, in part, on Israel has come, until the complement of the nations may be entering. And thus all Israel shall be saved, according as it is written, Arriving out of Zion shall be the Rescuer. He will be turning away irreverence from Jacob* (Romans 11:25,26).

God dealt with Israel for hundred's of years. He went to great lengths to prove to them and to all mankind that *by works of law, no flesh at all shall be justified in His sight* (Romans 3:20). Now is the time for Him to do a mighty work in all who believe from all nations.

*Or is He the God of the Jews only? Is He not of the nations also? Yes, of the nations also, if so be that God is One, Who will be justifying the Circumcision out of faith and the Uncircumcision through faith. Are we, then, nullifying law through faith? May it not be coming to that! Nay, we are sustaining law* (Romans 3:29-31).

This may surprise some, especially the pure grace believers but God is not nullifying the law during this time of dealing with the nations. In fact, through His operation in us we are sustaining law. Many saints stumble with how we can sustain law, in grace, through faith. We are sure it is not by concentrating on the precepts and working diligently to keep them. Only in the evangel of the grace of God do we find the happy clue.

*Being entombed together with Him in baptism, in Whom we were roused together also through faith in the operation of God, Who rouses Him from among the dead, we also being dead to the offenses and the uncircumcision of our flesh, He vivifies us together jointly with Him, dealing graciously with all our offenses, and has erased the handwriting of the decrees against us, which was hostile to us, and has taken it away nailing it to the cross* (Colossians 2:12-14).

Although, we did not literally die with Christ, nor are we literally roused yet, this truth is more than just a doctrine. Being identified with Christ in His death and resurrection, we are now said to be dead to our offenses and made alive to Christ. The decrees that were hostile to us, He took with Him, to the cross and thereby erased them. We are now exempted from the decrees of the law for a good reason. Not as some presume, for us to have a few years of fleeting fun in the flesh, but for us *to be **slaving in newness of spirit*** *and not in oldness of letter* (Romans 7:6).

*For the letter* [of the law] *is killing, yet the spirit is vivifying* (2Corinthians 3:6).

Being made alive in the spirit is man's crowning glory and far excels any temporary enjoyment of the flesh or any status or standing that the law could offer for even the most dedicated.

*If, then, you died together with Christ from the elements of the world* [the Mosaic system, Concordant Keyword, pg 87] *why, as living in the world, are you subject to decrees: You should not be touching, nor yet tasting, nor yet coming into contact, (which things are all for corruption from use), in accord with the directions and teachings of men? which are (having, indeed, an expression of wisdom in a willful ritual and humility and asceticism)* **not of any value toward the surfeiting of the flesh** (Colossians 2:20-23).

The fact that much of Christendom religiously attends to their pet rituals and ceremonies, is no proof that there is any value in them. When it comes to curbing the desires of the flesh, at best they can only produce an outward appearance or facade, of holiness.

*Beware of doing your good actions in the sight of men, in order to attract their gaze; if you do, there is no reward for you with your Father who is in Heaven. When you give in charity, never blow a trumpet before you as the hypocrites do in the synagogues and streets in order that their praises may be sung by men. I solemnly tell you that they already have their reward* (Matthew 6:1,2, Weymouth).

Regardless of how sincere one may be, in performing many religious rituals and ceremonies, they will not and cannot accomplish what they promise. They are an empty, endless, exercise in futility. In fact, all these outward props are a distraction and actually draw more attention to the flesh and away from Christ. It is very interesting to note that the elements of the Greek words translated "religion" and "religious" are DREAD – TEACH. (Concordant Keyword pg. 244) Dread and fear walk hand in hand but a love for God and His truth will conquer both.

## Holy and Flawless

*Blessed be the God and Father of our Lord Jesus Christ, Who blesses us with every spiritual blessing among the celestials, in Christ, according as He chooses us in Him before the disruption of the world, we to be **holy and flawless** in His sight, in love designating us beforehand for the place of a son for Him through Christ Jesus; in accord with the delight of His will, for the laud of the glory of His grace* (Ephesians 1:3-6).

One of our most precious spiritual blessings, which will bring applause to the glory of His grace, is realized in the promise that we were chosen by God to be holy and flawless in His sight. Although, we were chosen, in Christ, for this honor, before we were born, this also is much more than just a doctrine about our standing in Christ. Even if we can't understand how this will come to be, or why we were chosen, we must see that God has declared it and therefore holy and flawless we shall be.

## From the Day

God told Adam "in the day you eat from the tree of the knowledge of good and evil, **in that day**, to die shall you be dying" (Genesis 2:17). Adam did not succumb to death on that day but became mortal; the dying process began. 900+ years later he finally died. Likewise we have the promise that **from the day** we hear and realized the grace of God in truth, from that day the word will bear fruit in us and grow (Colossians 1:6). Also, from the day Paul heard that the Colossians believed the evangel and realized God's grace, he did not cease praying for them. His specific request had to do with the growing process of bearing fruit. God's work had begun in their heart and he prayed that it would be carried into effect in a practical way.

*From the day on which we hear, do not cease praying for you and requesting that you may be filled full with the realization of God's will, in all wisdom and spiritual understanding, you to walk worthily of the Lord for all pleasing, bearing fruit in every good work, and growing in the realization of God; being endued with all power, in accord with the might of His glory, for all endurance and patience with joy. At the same time giving thanks to the Father, Who makes us competent for a part of the allotment of the saints, in light* (Colossians 1:9-12).

The realization of God's grace triggers the new life process in us as Adam's disobedience started the dying process. We become a new creation from the day we believe and are baptized into Christ by the spirit (2 Corinthians 5:17).

*If the spirit of Him Who rouses Jesus from among the dead is making its home in you, He Who rouses Christ Jesus from among the dead will also be* **vivifying your mortal bodies** *because of His spirit making its home in you* (Romans 8:11).

The process of being made alive beyond the reach of death, begins in our mortal bodies as the opposite effect started in Adam's body. We know the process will not be completed until we are changed and our mortality puts on immortality (1 Corinthians 15:53) but the process has begun nonetheless.

It may be helpful to view being made holy and flawless as a process, also that will be completed when we are changed. Paul's prayer reveals the process. A **realization of God's will**, in all wisdom and spiritual understanding comes first. A worthy **walk**, pleasing to the Lord and **bearing fruit follows.** As we daily grow in the realization of God in our lives we are **endued with power,** in accord with the might of His glory for all **endurance** and **patience with joy** and at the same time our hearts are filled with thanksgiving to the Father, Who makes us competent.

The impact of this blessing may not be evident to those around us and there are many days we don't see growth in ourselves. It is good to remind ourselves that our expectation of putting on immortality, as well as being made competent for a part of the allotment of the saints is based on His ability to fulfill His clear declaration. It is not dependent on what we can see with our natural eyes. *Expectation, being observed, is not expectation* (Romans 8:24). His just ones have always walked by faith and have always been saved daily through faith.

*Faith is an assumption of what is being expected, a conviction concerning matters, which are not being observed* (Hebrews 11:1).

We are in the process of becoming blameless *children of God, flawless, in the midst of a generation crooked among whom we are appearing as luminaries in the world* (Philippians 2:15). Daily *stripping off the old humanity together with its practices, and putting on the young,* assures us that the *new creation is being renewed into recognition,* through us, *to accord with the Image of the One Who creates it* (Colossians 3:9,10).

## Cause and Effect

The God and Father of our Lord Jesus Christ as the Supreme Deity is the "First Cause" of all. He is the One, Who is *operating all in accord with the counsel of His will* (Ephesians 1:11). No one gives to Him first, seeing that *out of Him and through Him and for Him is all* (Romans 11:35,36). Behind the scenes, *God is working all together for the good of those who love God, those who are called according to His purpose* (Romans 8:28).

The effect, of His works, is manifested in many different ways throughout His vast universe. God's operation of grace, reigning in His saints, is not only according to His will but also for the sake of His delight (Philippians 2:13). It brings Him great pleasure to live and move in His children. He is the invisible, unseen cause behind any and all outward, visible progress we make in walking in love. We have this confidence that *He, Who undertakes a good work among us, will be performing it until the day of Jesus Christ* (1:6). He has promised and He will accomplish it.

The elements of the Greek word translated promise are ON-MESSAGE. Promise is to profess a course of conduct. (Concordant keyword, pg.233) The joy of our salvation today and the glorious expectation of something better tomorrow are both grounded "on the message", which is God's power for salvation. The good news of the grace of God cannot fail. For the Son of God, Jesus Christ, Who is being heralded among us,

*became not "Yes and "No, but in Him has become "Yes." Whatever promises are of God, are in Him "Yes." Wherefore through Him also is the "Amen" to God, for glory, through us. Now He Who is confirming us together with you in Christ, and anoints us, is God, Who also seals us and is giving the earnest* [or pledge] *of the spirit in our hearts* (2Corinthians 1:19-22).

"God's promises are not like those of His servants, but are always confirmed in Christ. He is not only able to carry out His will, but His promises are made with a full knowledge of all conditions such as might arise to change the course of one of His servants. They [His servants] are fallible, He is infallible . . . We are anointed with the spirit, as Christ, the Anointed, was at His baptism. This qualifies us for service. The seal is the sign of possession. We belong to God. The earnest is that small installment of the spirit, which we have received, which is the pledge of its fullness in the day of deliverance." – (Concordant Commentary, pg. 267, 268)

We have His spirit within and we have His word without, as our guide. By becoming acquainted with the sacred scriptures we are made wise for salvation through faith, which is in Christ Jesus. He is the Inaugurator (author, Young's Literal) of our faith and He is also the Perfecter (Hebrews 12:2,). Between God's operation of beginning a good work among us, and His operation of completing this work, is our, seemingly insignificant but vital part, which is listening and obeying from the heart the teaching of the evangel.

## We Should be Cleansing Ourselves

*The solid foundation of God stands, having this seal: The Lord knew those who are His, and, Let everyone who is naming the name of the Lord withdraw from injustice. Now in a great house there are not only gold and silver utensils, but wooden and earthenware also, and some indeed for honor, yet some for dishonor.* **If, then, anyone should ever be purging himself** *from these, he will be a utensil for honor, hallowed, and useful to the Owner, made ready for every good act. Now youthful desires flee: yet pursue righteousness, faith, love, peace, with all who are invoking the Lord out of a clean heart* (2Timothy 2:19-22).

The entreaty is plain: withdraw from injustice, **purge yourself** in order to become a vessel of honor and useful to our Owner. It is folly to think otherwise. How can we begin to understand what "purging ourselves" means if we ignore the entreaty on the basis that we are already holy and flawless in God's sight? Let us consider a companion passage and phrase.

*Do not become diversely yoked with unbelievers. . . You are the temple of the living God, according as God said, that I will be making My home and will be walking in them, and I will be their God, and they shall be My people. . . touch not the unclean, and*

*I will admit you, and I will be a Father to you, and you shall be sons and daughters to Me, says the Lord Almighty. Having, then, these promises, beloved, **we should be cleansing ourselves** from every pollution of flesh and spirit, completing holiness in the fear of God* (2Corinthians 6:14-7:1).

In the passage above we find a similar entreaty and phrase. Instead of *purging ourselves* we are now told that we should be *cleansing ourselves*. Let us pay close attention to the words preceding this second entreaty, *having then these promises, we should be cleansing ourselves*. The word "should" does not mean "we better do it or else". Neither does it mean that we ought to do it. It may be helpful to consider a brief study on the use of the words "may" and "should" in the Concordant Version. Dean Hough, in the Unsearchable Riches, vol. 81, page 267, wrote the following.

"Because the consequences of the cross are something expressed by verbs in the subjunctive mode, some have concluded there is an element of uncertainty about these consequences. To be sure, we cannot predict how the evangel will affect people today, but this does not make the results of the cross any less certain. Those who are believing and retaining the evangel (1Corinthians 15:2) as it relates to justification will be having peace toward God. . . . Why then does Paul use subjunctives in Romans 5:1? [Being, then, justified by faith, we may be having peace toward God, through our Lord, Jesus Christ] . . . It cannot be that he wished to express doubt about these blessings and glories that issue from the cross. Peace is the divine achievement made through the blood of the cross of the Son of God's love (Colossians 1:20).

The Greek subjunctive does not imply ought (see Keyword Concordance, p.268, under the word "should"). The word "subjunctive" itself means "subjoined" or "subordained"; it is dependent on some other action. In many contexts where the Greek subjunctive is used, we can find statements in the indicative mode that provide the basis for the subjunctive statement . . . those who are believing that Jesus our Lord was roused because of our justifying (Romans 4:24,25) will be having peace toward God (5:1) . . . The use of the present subjunctive verb, "may be having peace," again directs us to search for its basis. Our awareness of this good news of justification, our retaining of the evangel which tells of God's achievement in the blood of the cross and our believing that we are justified is bound to instill peace in our hearts towards God." End of quote.

Let us look closer at the use of the verb in the subjunctive mode in the statement we are considering from 2Corinthians 7:1, "*We should be cleansing ourselves from every pollution of flesh and spirit, completing holiness in the fear of God*". The verb "should" directs us to search for the basis of how this is possible. How should we, or how can we **cleanse ourselves**? The preceding statement to which this is subjoined is the basis of our expectation. It is, "*having then these promises beloved*".

By faith we accept the promise that God has made His home in us. We are in awe that He is now walking in us and is our God (2Corinthians 6:16). Our part is to separate ourselves from the darkness and be severed, hallowed or set apart for the Lord (:17). Not literally, or we would have to come out of the world, but in spirit, motive and purpose.

To be chosen, hand picked out of billions and set apart by God and for Him is the highest honour we will ever receive on earth. A revelation of this fact will change our outlook on our service to the Lord. As we obey from the heart and touch not the unclean, He continually draws closer and admits us (literally INTO-RECEIVE, Concordant Keyword pg.10) and is a Father to us (:18).

Growing in this realization is the powerful motivation behind the process enabling us to *cleanse ourselves from every pollution of flesh and spirit.* This is how we *complete holiness in the fear of God* (7:1).

By communing with our Lord listening to and believing the living declarations from the One Who does not and cannot lie, we shall, indeed be cleansing ourselves and be completing holiness. **Grace working in us** through Christ, the living word, **is the power** on which we rely in completing holiness. We are continually and vitally involved in this life long on going operation of the spirit in our heart.

Paul continues in this passage and gives details of how the ecclesia at Corinth cleansed themselves completely regarding the specific problem he had addressed in his first letter.

*Now I am rejoicing, not that **you were made sorry**, but that you were made sorry **to repentance**. For you were made sorry according to God, that in nothing you may suffer forfeit by us. For sorrow according to God is producing repentance for unregretted salvation, yet the sorrow of the world is producing death. For lo! this same thing-for you to made sorry according to God - how much it produces in you of diligence, nay, defense, nay, resentment, nay, fear, nay, longing, nay, zeal, nay, avenging! In everything **you commend yourselves to be pure in this matter*** (:9-11).

The cleansing process may mean we are made sorry, time and again. Not according to the sorrow of the world but a Godly sorrow that leads to repentance, a change of mind and a *renewing of our mind* (Romans 12:2). This is a practical example of how grace works in the life of a believer as we walk in spirit in intimate communion, retaining the truth of the evangel.

The promises are in accord with the evangel, which is God's power to those who believe them. The power is in the message of promise and expectation because of what the cross of Christ has accomplished and is the basis for how we cleanse ourselves and carry our salvation into effect.

Jesus told His disciples,

*I am the true Grapevine, and My Father is the Farmer. Every branch in Me bringing forth no fruit, He is taking it away, and every one bringing forth fruit, **He is cleansing it**, that it may be bringing forth more fruit. **Remain in Me**. I also am in you. According as the branch can not be bringing forth fruit from itself, if it should not be remaining in the grapevine, thus neither you, if you should not remain in Me* (John 15:1-4).

## Presenting to Himself a Glorious Ecclesia

Another example of the Greek subjunctive mood and the use of the words "should" and "may" is found in Ephesians and directly applies to our present topic.

*Christ loves the ecclesia, and gives Himself up for its sake, that He **should be** hallowing it* [setting it apart], *cleansing it in the bath of the water (with His declaration), that He **should be** presenting to Himself a glorious ecclesia, not having spot or wrinkle or any such things, but that it **may be** holy and flawless* (Ephesians 5:25-27).

Christ's love, and the giving of Himself for the ecclesia is the basis for Him hallowing and cleansing us. The bath of the water that cleanses is His declaration. *Being justified by faith, we **may be** having peace toward God, through our Lord, Jesus Christ* (Romans 5:1). Being justified is the basis that we surely have peace. Likewise, the fact that He is setting us apart and cleansing us, is the basis on which He shall present to Himself a glorious ecclesia, holy and flawless.

Further, receiving and holding to these promises, in spirit, is the basis on which we are cleansing ourselves and completing holiness. We are now free to walk in His love, by faith, clinging to the promise that He will complete the work He has begun.

## Be Imitators of God,

How far should we carry this train of thought? Not further than our apostle. Paul did not stop being the pattern of those about to be saved after his Damascus Road experience. In his later years he exhorts all saints to *Become imitators of me, according as I also am of Christ* (1Corinthians 11:1). He even went so far as to instruct us,

*Become, then, imitators of God, as beloved children, and be walking in love* (Ephesians 5:1,2)

We are related to God; we are His offspring and therefore will we not resemble Him? *If anyone is in Christ, there is a new creation: the primitive passed by* (2Corinthians 5:17). This transformation from old to new was obvious in Paul; he went from the chief of sinners to a chief apostle and is our pattern during this administration of grace. As imitators of God, walking in love, we of all people should live the most exemplary lives.

*As children of light be walking (for the fruit of the light is in all goodness and righteousness and truth), testing what is well pleasing to the Lord* (Ephesians 5:9,10).

*Therefore He is saying, 'Rouse! O drowsy one, and rise from among the dead, and Christ shall dawn upon you!' Be observing accurately, then, brethren, how you are walking, not as unwise, but as wise, reclaiming the era, for the days are wicked. Therefore do not become imprudent, but understand what the will of the Lord is* (:14-17).

We live in a dark, wicked age and like all mankind, suffer pain and sorrow. The evil we face daily is not a token of God's displeasure. Evil is God's temporary servant and serves His purpose as a necessary contrast for the display of good. As painful as it is for us, it is even more so for our loving Father. But God knows that without the darkness of this wicked age His righteousness and the word of life in us will not be visible. The glory of the stars cannot be seen at noonday. On the darkest night is their splendor most visible; only then is a sense of God's vast universe realized. With this understanding let us continue to pray for endurance and patience with joy.

*And be not drunk with wine, in which is profligacy, but be filled full with spirit, speaking to yourselves in psalms and hymns and spiritual songs, singing and playing music in your hearts to the Lord, giving thanks always for all things, in the name of our Lord, Jesus Christ, to our God and Father, being subject to one another in the fear of Christ* (:18-21).

*At the same time giving thanks to the Father, Who makes you competent for a part of the allotment of the saints, in light, Who rescues us out of the jurisdiction of Darkness, and transports us into the kingdom of the Son of His love* (Colossians 1:12,13).

We are no longer a part of the darkness; God has rescued us out of its jurisdiction. Therefore we are not to participate in the *unfruitful acts of darkness,* yet rather as *children of light* we are to *be exposing them* (Ephesians 5:8-11). God is in the process of making us competent for a part of the future allotment of the **saints in light**. Yet even now He calls to wake up and be filled with spirit and let our light shine in the midst of the necessary darkness all around us.  In a very real sense **we are the light of the world.**

*A city located upon a mountain can not be hid. Thus **let shine your light in front of men,** so that they may perceive your ideal acts and should glorify your Father Who is in the heavens (Matthew 5:14-16).*

*Love is not working evil to an associate. **The complement, then, of law, is love.** This, also, do, being aware of the era, that it is already the hour for us to be roused out of sleep, for now is our salvation nearer than when we believe. The night progresses, yet the day is near. We, then, should be putting off the acts of darkness, yet should **be putting on the implements** (or weapons, AV. armour) **of light**. As in the day, respectably, should we be walking, not in revelries and drunkenness, not in chambering and wantonness, not in strife and jealousy, but **put on the Lord Jesus Christ,** and be making no provision for the lusts of the flesh.* (Romans13:10-14)

# CHAPTER 6

## Christ is Our Salvation

### Our Present Salvation is a Relationship

From the outset we emphatically asserted that God is the First Cause behind every aspect of our salvation. **God's love** for mankind, **God's desire** to save all of His creatures, and **His ability** to do so, are foundational truths that all else is built on. This is the rock on which we must establish our complete belief system regarding our salvation past, present or future. Salvation is not out of us, it is God's approach present. We must now add, that when it is all said and done, Christ Himself is our salvation!

*Christ loves you, and **gives Himself** up for us, an approach present, and a sacrifice to God, for a fragrant odor* (Ephesians 5:2).

*We are hallowed* (pronounced holy and set apart for him) *through the approach present of the body of Jesus Christ once for all time* (Hebrews 10:10).

There was a God-fearing man, in Jerusalem named Simeon, who waited long for Israel's consolation. Finally, at a very old age, Joseph and Mary brought the little child Jesus to the temple to present Him to the Lord. The old man, Simeon took Him up in his arms and proclaimed he was now ready to die in peace because his eyes had seen *God's salvation* (Luke 2:27-30).

## Our Salvation is a Person

Christ is the Savior of the world; He, Himself **is** *the power of God and the wisdom of God* (1Corinthians 1:24). He also *became to us wisdom from God, besides righteousness and holiness and deliverance* (:30).

*The One not knowing sin, God makes to be a sin offering for our sakes that we may be becoming God's righteousness in Him* (2Corinthians 5:21).

Jesus came that we may *have life eonian, and have it superabundantly* (John 10:10). His spirit is our guiding light, our comforter and our best friend. Not only is He the love of our life; Christ, actually is our Life and when He shall be manifested, then we also *shall be manifested together with Him in glory* (Colossians 3:4). *In Him we live and move and are* (Acts 17:28). He is our all and *in Him we are complete* (Colossians 2:10). Our salvation is a relationship with the Lord Jesus Christ.

## Two Great Secrets

Two secrets in scripture are called great. As an introduction to the one secret in Ephesians chapter five we read,

*Husbands, be loving your wives according **as Christ also loves the ecclesia*** (Ephesians 5:25).

The love of Christ is a powerful force and so underestimated! He loves us and cherishes us the way we cherish our own body.

*For no one at any time hates his own flesh, but is nurturing and cherishing it, according as Christ also the ecclesia, for **we are members of His body*** (:29,30).

A man, who falls in love with a woman, is driven by an unseen force within, and eagerly, often recklessly, leaves his father and mother and will do all in his power to be joined to his woman. When a marriage is consummated the two become one flesh and share a special intimacy. Often, the miraculous result is a new life. God blessed this union so man would *be fruitful, increase and fill the earth, and subdue it* (Genesis 1:28). This secret is great: yet Paul was portraying the union of a man and a woman as a picture of Christ and His ecclesia (Ephesians 5:32).

## To Know the Love of Christ

We have written about the power of grace compared to the weakness of the flesh. We have gloried in our high position in Christ and our future heavenly allotment. God has begun a work far above and beyond anything we can imagine. However, there is a way, in spirit, to enter into this realm, where God is operating, which is beyond our understanding. It is through an intimate love relationship with our Lord and Savior. Words fail to do this union justice. We have to experience it for ourselves. An awareness of Christ's love will give us the courage to face a lion's den or a fiery furnace and the strength to follow Him regardless of the cost or danger.

Long before the administration of the grace of God or *"the dispensation of the spirit"* (2Corinthians 3:8) King David, the *"man according to God's Own heart"*, (Acts 13:22) craved God's love and entered into a closeness with Him more precious than his life itself. He wrote,

*My God, My soul thirsts for You. My flesh craves for You, like a land arid and faint, without water. So longing, in the Sanctuary, I envisioned You, Beholding Your strength and Your glory; For Your mercy and bounty are **better than life itself**. My lips, they*

*shall laud You. So shall I bless You in all my life. As with fatness and richness my soul shall be satisfied, And with jubilant lips my mouth shall praise. When I remember You on my berth, In night vigils shall I soliloquize* (talk to myself) *about You. And in the shadow of Your wings shall I be jubilant.* **My soul clings to You;** *Your right hand upholds me* (Psalm 63:1-8).

Now that Christ has taken His abode in us, it must be that we can have an even closer bond with Him than David experienced. Jesus speaking to His Father said,

*I have given them the glory which Thou has given Me, that they may be one, according as We are One, I in them and Thou in Me* (John 17:22,23).

The reality of our oneness with Christ, sharing His glory and love, is better than life itself. One does not dwell long in the reality of His love, for this spiritual realm to become more real to us  than the physical. Although, unknown to the masses, what each and every child of God has to experience for himself, is the fact that during our darkest hour God's love is most realized. The more desperate our need; the closer His presence is realized. Our hearts need to be broken; that's how the light gets in; that's how His love gets in. Paul learned this lesson well.

## Afflictions Produce Glory

*Fully follow me in my teaching, motive, purpose, faith, patience, love, endurance, persecutions, sufferings* (2Timothy 3:10,11).

Although, most of us will never be called on to experience the hardships Paul did, yet we are to fully follow his example. The inspired order of his list starts with the entreaty to follow him in his teaching and ends in following him in his suffering.

Each aspect represents a deeper level of commitment, maturity and closeness. God's direct route through the wilderness is the way we grow in the realization of His grace and His will. With each step comes the opportunity to know Him and to experience His love that passes understanding in a new way. This is what Paul wrote about his life of constant troubles.

*In everything, being afflicted, but not distressed; perplexed, but not despairing; persecuted, but not forsaken; cast down, but not perishing - always carrying about in the body the deadening of Jesus, that the life also of Jesus may be manifested in our body* (2Corinthians 4:8-10)

The deadening of our body comes before the life of Jesus can be manifested in us. A few verses later he expounded on how the afflictions and the dying process of mortality in general is working in our favor, and for the glory of God's grace, especially in the life yet to come.

*Wherefore we are not despondent, but even if our outward man is decaying, nevertheless that within us is being renewed day by day. For the momentary lightness of **our affliction is producing** for us a transcendently transcendent eonian **burden of glory**, at our not noting what is being observed, but what is not being observed, for what is being observed is temporary, yet what is not being observed is eonian* (:16-18).

Our troubles here below cause us to turn our attention upward to our Lord seated at the right hand of the Father. The more desperate our need for His love, the more evident it will be. He is always near, and His love will reveal our afflictions, as they really are. In the face of eternity, they are **momentary and light.** There is glory just around the corner for us, relatively speaking. May we take comfort in the fact that God is using our afflictions to produce the glory yet ahead for us.

## Staunch with Power - Grounded in Love

An awareness of the love of Christ is our most precious possession. It provides a steadfast anchor in all our troubles and restrains an improper perspective to our so-called successes. This awareness has the power to change our life from an aimless struggle to a glorious expectation. His love is the pearl of great price not to be traded for all the gold in the world. Paul's prayer for us is this,

*That He [God] may be giving you, in accord with the riches of His glory, **to be made staunch with power**, through His spirit, in the man within, Christ to dwell in our hearts through faith, that we, **having been rooted and grounded in love**, should be strong to grasp, together with all the saints, what is the breadth and length and depth and height - to know the love of Christ as well which transcends knowledge - that we may be **completed for the entire complement of God*** (Ephesians 3:16-19).

Christ dwells in our hearts by faith. Through His spirit we are being made staunch with power. The hard trials and the corresponding dependency on God's grace and love cause the eyes of our heart to perceive the transcendent revelations on a deeper level. Being rooted and grounded in His love is the only way to be made strong enough to grasp, together with all the saints, the deep revelations of the spirit. Only through eyes of love, so to speak, can we get to know the way we *must know*. Also, *if anyone is loving God, this one is known by Him* (1Corinthians 8:2,3), in a way that others are not yet known.

Likewise, in order to be completed for the entire complement of God, we must know the love of Christ intimately, which transcends all mental perceptions. This takes place in the heart, the core and center of our spiritual being. Spiritual revelations must be taught by the spirit. Communicating them effectively with human words falls so short. Each of us **must experience them** for ourselves, one day at a time through living, under the shelter of Christ's love and God's grace.

Although, the love of Christ is beyond our mind's ability to understand, our hearts know it well. A continual growing realization of God's operation in us provides the endurance and patience with joy that we need for today. Tomorrow will take care of itself in the same manner. Slowly the reality sinks in that we don't need to do anything to win God's favor. There is nothing we can do to cause Him to love us more than He already does. Walking worthily, our acceptable, divine, service is simply a spontaneous response to the love of Christ. We love Him and cheerfully serve Him only because He continually, unceasingly, first loves us. Day by day according to our need the love of God is being *poured into our hearts through the holy spirit, which is being given to us* (Romans 5:5). To know the love of Christ is the way to live life to the fullest.

## Put on The Panoply (Armour) of God

*For the rest, brethren mine, be invigorated in the Lord and in the might of His strength. Put on the panoply of God, to enable you to stand up to the stratagems of the Adversary, for it is not ours to wrestle with blood and flesh, but with the sovereignties, with the authorities, with the world-mights of this darkness, with the spiritual forces of wickedness among the celestials. Therefore take up the panoply of God that you may be enabled to withstand in the wicked day, and having effected all, to stand. Stand, then, girded about your loins with truth, with the cuirass of righteousness put on and your feet sandaled with the readiness of the evangel of peace; with all taking up the large shield of faith, by which you will be able to extinguish all the fiery arrows of the wicked one. And receive the helmet of salvation and the sword of the spirit, which is a declaration of God* (Ephesians 6:10-17).

It is not coincidence that Paul discusses the panoply (lit. EVERY-IMPLEMENT) or the **armour of God** at the end of the book of Ephesians. Once the eyes of our heart have been enlightened to see the glory of our calling, and what the Lord has prepared for us, and our hearts have been blessed to know the love of Christ, then we are ready to begin to take up the weapons of our warfare.

*For walking in the flesh, not according to the flesh do we war, for the weapons of our warfare are not fleshly, but powerful to God for bringing down of strongholds, reasonings bringing down, and every high thing lifted up against the knowledge of God, and bringing into captivity every thought to the obedience of the Christ* (2Corinthians 10:3-5, Young's Literal).

## The Stratagems of the Adversary

The purpose of putting on the panoply of God is to be able to *stand up to the stratagems of the Adversary* (Ephesians 6:10). A stratagem is a systematizing, a method of procedure, of the enemy. (Concordant Keyword pg. 298) We are in a spiritual warfare; because we have an invisible enemy some may not even recognize the need for protection.

The goal of the enemy is to get God's people, to occupy their time with ceremonies and programs or in endless reasoning and human philosophy, anything to distract us from putting on God's armour. Many saints have also been influenced by a modern "Prosperity Gospel", which claims that the large shield of faith is to acquire wealth, happiness and success in this life.

The fiery arrows of the wicked one are seldom recognized as such and so the need to extinguish them and the ability to do so is not taken serious.

## Girded with Truth

The first means of defense is to gird our loins with spiritual truth that cannot be learned from a manual or in a classroom but that which the spirit must reveal to our hearts through the living word. The revelations we have discussed, many from the book of Ephesians, comprise powerful truths that will protect our minds and also gird our loins. Our loins are that region of the body between the ribs and the legs, figuratively the generative organs. (Concordant Keyword, pg. 182) God's truth protects our loins from the enemy's lies so the seeds of the word planted deep in a soft heart can grow and bear fruit. Truth received and loved will regenerate and flourish, reproducing more of its kind. To him who has, more will be given.

## The Cuirass of Righteousness

The second weapon of our warfare listed is the cuirass of righteousness. This is more than a breastplate, that only covers our front, as the Authorized Version translates it. The cuirass is a corselet or double breastplate, protecting the body from the neck to the waist . (Concordant Keyword, pg. 64) The only other place Paul mentions a cuirass is in Thessalonians.

*We, being of the day, may be sober, putting on the **cuirass of faith and love**, and the helmet, the expectation of salvation, for God did not appoint us to indignation, but to the procuring of salvation through our Lord Jesus Christ, Who died for our sakes,* *that, whether we may be watching or drowsing, we should be living together with Him* (1Thessalonians 5:8-10).

In this passage instead of being called a cuirass of righteousness it is now referred to as a cuirass of faith and love. Righteousness is thus equated with faith and love. We may be sober and put on the cuirass of faith and love because God has appointed us for salvation. As a testimony to the fact that we are saved in grace, Paul adds, whether we watch or drowse, we will be living with Christ. From the day one realizes the grace of God in truth they begin to bear the fruit of righteousness (Colossians 1:6). Only grace can overwhelm with faith and love (1Timothy 1:14). The good news of grace is the power of God for salvation.

The legalists is mistaken thinking God chose him for salvation because he believes and walks righteously. The fatalist reasons that because God choose him and saved in grace, it matters not if he watches or sleeps; either way he will still live with Christ. Both hold part of the truth; in grace, through faith, those of the day will put on the cuirass of righteousness and the helmet of salvation because God has appointed them to salvation.

Christ is our righteousness; to put on Christ is to put the truth, we hold dear, into practice, because or on the basis that this is what we are appointed to do. Paul's exhortation to the ecclesia at Philippi was this,

**What you learned** and accepted and hear and perceived in me, these **be putting into practice** (Philippians 4:9).

Paul *talked the talk* but he also *walked the walk*. He is not asking the Philippians to do something he did not do himself. They had not only heard and accepted the good news message given to Paul but witnessed a living expression of it in his life, also. He now asks them and us to put into practice what we have learned from him and observed in him.

## Do Not Worry about Anything

A tree is known by its fruit. Likewise, false teachings, under the cloak of "pure grace", or otherwise, can only bring forth of their own kind and will eventually be exposed, for what they are. If doctrines produce the fruit of apathy and fatalism something is amiss. Pet phrases repeated out of context such as "**All is of God**" (1Corinthians 11:12, 2Corinthians 5:18) tend to tickle the ears of the drowsing saints but accomplish little else. I agree that we can take great consolation in the fact that, absolutely speaking; God is in control of all and is operating all in accord with His will (Ephesians 1:11). However, picking out isolated phrases such as "do not worry about anything" (:6) without considering the context can be misleading and destructive.

What is often meant by do not worry about anything is we do not need to get involved in anything because "all is of God". The peace of God is reduced to indifference and unconcern in a "whatever will be will be" attitude. By considering a few verses where this phrase is found will make it obvious that this is a relative truth based on other facts clearly stated in the passage and applicable to our subject at hand. We must see the basis for the entreaty not to worry about anything.

*So that, my brethren, beloved and longed for, my joy and wreath, **be standing firm** thus in the Lord, my beloved . . .. Be rejoicing in the Lord always! Again, I will declare, be rejoicing! Let your lenience be known to all men: the Lord is near. Do not worry about anything, but in **everything, by prayer** and petition, with thanksgiving, **let your requests be made known** to God, and the peace of God, that is superior to every frame of mind, shall be garrisoning your hearts and your apprehensions in Christ Jesus. . . **What you learned** also, and accepted and hear and perceived in me, these **be putting into practice**, and the God of peace will be with you* (Philippians 4:1-7).

During our daily struggles and afflictions we can stand firm, rejoicing in the Lord, knowing God is in control and always has a purpose in mind and is working all for our good (Romans 8:28). Our *affliction is producing endurance, yet endurance testedness* (Romans 5:3,4). Worry accomplishes nothing; neither does apathy and indifference, for that matter. We are not to worry about anything but we are to do something else; instead of worrying or running from our problems we are to face them head on with prayer and petition. There is a way we are enabled to not worry about **anything; it** is by praying about **everything**.

## The God of Peace – The Peace of God

From Philippians 4 we quoted two similar thoughts, *"the peace of God . . . shall be garrisoning your hearts"*(:7) and *"the God of peace will be with you"* (:9). The first is based on praying and the second on putting into practice what we have learned. We must assume therefore, relatively speaking, that those who do not pray should not expect His peace to protect their heart.

Likewise, those who do not put the truth they have received into practice, should not assume the God of peace will not be with them. Not that they lose their salvation but that they lose the joy and reality of God's closeness and the awareness of His ever present love. If this were not the case what would be the point of the exhortations "to pray" and "to put into practice"?

*The **weapons** of our warfare are not fleshly, but **powerful** to God toward the pulling down of bulwarks; pulling down reckonings and every height elevating itself against the knowledge of God, and leading into captivity every apprehension into the **obedience of Christ** (2Corinthians 10:4,5).*

Absolutely speaking, the God of peace will never leave us, for *in*

*Him we are living and moving and are* (Acts 17:28) but we can't enjoy His peace walking in stubbornness, either in active rebellion or passive indifference. If all the great secrets and revelations we claim to understand are not in accord with the other "great secret", *the secret of devoutness*, (1Timothy 3:16), we should be suspicious of their worth and source. We are not exempt from the light in us, becoming darkness (Luke 11:35).

It should go without saying; if we do not acknowledge the Lord and look to Him with a thankful and submissive heart in **everything,** neither should we expect the ability to not worry? Our awareness of His abiding spirit, leading us on, gives us the assurance that He is near and He not only hears our prayer but His spirit is actually doing the praying through us (Romans 8:26). Therefore we do not worry but rejoice and rest in the peace that comes from knowing Him. In this way the **God of peace** is with us and the **peace of God** protects us.

## Pray on Every Occasion

Real prayer is not to obey a decree or to exercise a religious ritual. Prayer is communion with our God and Saviour. There are so many exhortations in the scriptures, especially from our apostle Paul regarding prayer that it is almost unthinkable that the enemy has managed to almost make it a non- issue.

There is only one way to learn how to pray and that is to pray. Through the process of consciously depending on God, making requests, with thanksgiving, that the peace of God protects our minds, like a military force. Prayer becomes a way of life, a continual awareness of God's love, comfort and His promise of deliverance and provision. I cannot see any other way to understand and obey from the heart the many entreaties to pray on every occasion, in everything and without ceasing. I will quote a few for those who may not be familiar with them. There are many more and a worthy study on its own.

*Have fond affection for one another with brotherly fondness, in honor deeming one another first, in diligence not slothful, **fervent** in spirit, slaving for the Lord, rejoicing in expectation, enduring affliction, **persevering in prayer*** (Romans 12:10-12).

*During every prayer and petition **be praying on every occasion** (in spirit **being vigilant** also for it **with all perseverance** and petition concerning all the saints* (Ephesians 6:18).

***In prayer be persevering**, watching in it with thanksgiving* (Colossians 4:2).

By dwelling in the realm of grace, glorying the evangel of grace, and obeying from the heart the teachings we were given; we slowly but surely put on the mind of Christ. Our thought patterns, our heart's desires and longings become one with the spirit's continual prayer in us and through us to God. The spirit has the ability to arrest our fears, doubts and apprehensions and bring them into the obedience of Christ.

## Truth, Which Accords with Devoutness

*Exercise yourself in devoutness* (1Timothy 4:7).

Devoutness is literally WELL-REVERence. (Concordant Keyword pg.74) To revere is to fear, feel awe, to regard with deep respect and love; venerate. (Webster's Dictionary) A genuine realization of the love and grace of God in truth will have an effect on our message and method of conduct. For either to be effective, they must be,

*In accord with the faith of God's chosen and a realization of the* **truth, which accords with devoutness** (Titus 1:1).

"We can not conjure up devoutness. Rather, devoutness will come naturally to the heart that dwells on the grace of our Savior, God." (Dean Hough, Unsearchable Riches vol.63, p38)

Whoever, are mature, are disposed to one thing. They have one goal in mind; pursuing the prize of God's calling above in Christ Jesus. (Philippians 3:13-15). Maturity produces a healthy fear of God, a holy awe and respect for Him and His calling. Our apostle had strong words for those who teach otherwise.

*If anyone is teaching differently and is not approaching with* **sound words,** *even those* **of our Lord Jesus Christ,** *and the teaching* **in accord with devoutness,** *he is conceited, versed in nothing, but morbid about questionings and controversies, out of which is coming envy, strife, calumnies, wicked suspicions, altercations of men of a decadent mind and deprived of the truth, inferring that devoutness is capital. Now devoutness with contentment is great capital* (1Timothy 6:3-6).

## The Readiness of the Evangel of Peace

The third piece of armor is for our feet. They need to be sandaled to walk with the evangel. This does not happen until after the first two are put on. Having knowledge of God's revelations is great but tends to puff up. Love alone can build up (1Corinthians 8:1). If we perceive all secrets, have all knowledge yet have no love, we are nothing (1Corinthians 13:2). Truth is necessary, else we are wasting our time studying and writing; putting on Christ, our righteousness is also compulsory to prepare any and all to proclaim the evangel of the grace of God.

We are, *deputies of Christ, and **administrators of God's secrets**. Here, furthermore, it is being sought in administrators that any such may be found faithful* (1Corinthians 4:1,2).

The message is truly wonderful.

*God was in Christ, conciliating the world to Himself, not reckoning their offenses to them, and placing in us the word of the conciliation. **For Christ**, then, **are we ambassadors**, as of God entreating through us. We are beseeching for Christ's sake, "Be conciliated to God!"* (2Corinthians 5:19,20).

If our lives are not **a living expression of love and conciliation** to those we heralding, our words will be little more than a clanging cymbal (1Corithians 13:1).

*Thanks be to God, Who always gives us a triumph in Christ, and is **manifesting** the odor of **His knowledge through us** in every place, for we are a fragrance of Christ to God, in those who are being saved and in those who are perishing: to these, indeed, an odor of death for death, yet to those an odor of life for life. And **for this who is competent**? For we are not as the majority, who are peddling the word of God, but as of sincerity, but as of God, in the sight of God in Christ, are we speaking* (2Corinthians 2:14-17).

## Who is Competent

Who is competent to herald the evangel? Apparently in Paul's day the majority were not. They were not sincere, nor were they even called of God. They were actually *peddling the word of God*, which is to sell at retail, with the insinuation of improper profit, either by overcharging or adulterating. (Concordant Keyword pg. 220)

To adulterate the word of God is to mix it with worthless elements. (Concordant Keyword pg. 10) I am not convinced that things have changed much.

The message of Christ crucified is not complicated but who is competent to imitate the apostle who was given the powerful message? He is our model (Philippians 3:7). His instructions to those who would follow him are,

*Herald the word. Stand by it, opportunely, inopportunely, expose, rebuke, entreat, with all patience and teaching. For the era will be when they will not tolerate sound teaching, but, their hearing being tickled, they will heap up for themselves teachers in accord with their own desires* (2Timothy 4:2,3).

Standing by the word involves entreaty and exposing and rebuking. This may be "tough love" but it is love, nonetheless.

## The Large Shield of Faith

*The just one by faith shall be living* (Romans 1:17, Galatians 3:11, Hebrews 10:38).

The next piece of armour we are to take up is *the large shield of faith, by which we will be able to extinguish all the fiery arrows of the wicked one* (Ephesians 6:16). Along with all the armour we **put on**, we also need to **take up** a shield, a large shield, the *large shield of faith*.

Once we have our feet sandaled and are ready to herald the evangel we will definitely become the target of the enemy and will be severely tested. Without genuine faith we will not be able to extinguish the fiery arrows of the wicked one and will quickly become discouraged and disillusioned.

There will be days we doubt that God is really in control of all, least of all our personal lives. Circumstances will appear to be out of control. At these times, especially, retaining the evangel and meditating on the promises may be our only source of endurance and patience with joy. If we place our confidence in ourselves or in anything other than the power of God's grace the arrows of doubt and fear will get through and cause havoc in our mind and life.

## Believe on the Lord Jesus, and you Shall be Saved

*Now you **be remaining in what you learned** and verified, being aware from whom you learned it, and that from a babe you are acquainted with the sacred scriptures, which are able to **make you wise for salvation through faith** which is in Christ Jesus. All scripture is inspired by God, and is beneficial for teaching, for **exposure**, for **correction**, for **discipline** in righteousness, that the man of God may be equipped, fitted out for every good act* (2Timothy 3:14-17).

Only the holy scriptures are able to make one wise **through faith**. Therefore, those who believe the scriptures and remain in them will be made wise. Likewise regarding the entreaties, we have been speaking of; they will be beneficial only if we take them to heart, and allow them to expose us, correct us and also discipline us in righteousness. God's way to be fitted out for every good work is through faith in His declarations. The word heard does not benefit hearers if it is not being *blended together with faith* (Hebrews 4:2).

When it comes to our present daily walk with the Lord, Paul's answer to the jailer at Philippi, may still apply to us today. It sums up the matter in the simplest terms possible. When asked, *"what must I be doing that I may be saved?"* Paul's answer was, *"believe on the Lord Jesus, and you shall be saved"* (Acts 16:30,31). There is absolutely no doubt that the evangel is God's power for salvation today but it is obvious that this is only true for those who actually believe the teachings in accord with the good news of the grace of God.

## Persisting in the Faith

*You, being once estranged and enemies in comprehension, by wicked acts, yet now He reconciles by His body of flesh, through His death, to present you **holy and flawless** and unimpeachable in His sight, since surely you are **persisting in the faith**, grounded and settled and are **not being removed from the expectation of the evangel** (Colossians 1:21-23).*

We all were once estranged and enemies in comprehension by our wicked acts. We are now holy and flawless in His sight since surely we are persisting in the faith grounded and settled, not being removed from the expectation of the evangel. To enjoy our salvation we must realize that the elevator to success is broken. We must use the stairs, one step at a time, daily taking up the large shield, persisting in the faith.

## When we are Weak, Then we are Powerful

We hold in our hearts a powerful message; good works are prepared ahead of time for us; we are called to get up each morning and walk in them by faith, believing the promises. It is not a matter of having all our doctrines down pat or being able to impress a few people with persuasive words of wisdom. It is rather, to be living the message of Christ crucified, in word and deed as a demonstration of spirit and of power. Our faith is not in the wisdom of men but in the power of God. We know we are weak and often walk in fear, and in much trembling. So did Paul.

*And **I came** to be with you **in weakness, and in fear,** and in much trembling, and my word and my heralding were not with the persuasive words of human wisdom, but with demonstration of spirit and of power, that your **faith** may not be in the wisdom of men but **in the power of God.*** (1Corinthians 2:3-5)

Our frailty is by God's design. *We are not heralding ourselves, but Christ Jesus the Lord, yet ourselves slaves because of Jesus. We have this treasure in earthen vessels that the transcendence of the power may be of God and not of us* (2Corinthians 4:5,7).

The more truth revealed to us the greater is our need to be aware of the weakness of our flesh, lest we get puffed up and forget that our sufficiency is of God. During the administration of the grace of God, Paul is our pattern (1Timothy 1:16). It is graciously granted for us to believe the revelations given to him and also to suffer for the same reason he did (Philippians 1:29). This is how he explained it.

*Lest I should be lifted up by the transcendence of the revelations, there was given to me a splinter in the flesh, a messenger of Satan, that he may be buffeting me, lest I may be lifted up. For this I entreat the Lord thrice, that it should withdraw from me. And He has protested to me, "Sufficient for you is My grace, for **My power in infirmity is being perfected**". With the greatest relish, then, will I rather be glorying in my infirmities, that the power of Christ should be tabernacling over me. Wherefore I delight in infirmities, in outrages, in necessities, in persecutions, in distresses, for Christ's sake, for, **whenever I may be weak, then I am powerful*** (2Corinthians 12:7-10).

The awareness of our own weakness causes us to rely on the living God and to depend on His grace, which is always sufficient for us. It is our constant awareness of God's grace and love that makes us powerful and causes the enemy's tactics to backfire. As we glory in our infirmities the power of Christ is our shelter.

## The Stratagems of the Adversary

*Put on the panoply of God, to enable you to stand up to the stratagems of the Adversary* (Ephesians 6:11).

We cannot over emphasize that God's panoply is to give us power to stand or to maintain an upright position. Without this armour the saints are helpless against the enemy, and may even be unaware of his tactics, his method of operation and their need to protect themselves.

*It is not ours to wrestle with blood and flesh, but with the sovereignties, with the authorities, with the world-mights of this darkness, with the spiritual forces of wickedness among the celestials* (:12).

Our warfare is not with people, regardless of how antagonistic they are. The inspired terms, "sovereignties, authorities, world-mights of darkness, and spiritual forces of wickedness among the celestials", more than suggest a vast and **powerful military regime**. They are invisible but they are real and have been actively fighting against the purpose and people of God since the beginning of time. It is futile to attempt to stand against them with fleshly weapons or to think that we will be competent to stand without being **invigorated, in the Lord** and the might of His strength (:10). Every implement is required to stand up to the stratagems of the Adversary, or to even see them for what they are, a well thought-out system of deception.

The verb *to put on*, referring to wearing the armour and the verb *to enable,* referring to our ability to stand are both in the middle voice. We do not perform this action on our own but neither does God automatically suit us with His armour. We cannot be passive about preparing for the war raging around us. We are involved, whether we like it or not, and need the armour to enable us to stand. The verb to stand is once again, in the incomplete or Act verb form. Wrestling and standing will be the on-going reality, in the life of every believer, until we die.

Effecting all to stand becomes a way of life for all saints pursuing the goal for the prize of God's calling above in Christ Jesus. Our high calling in Christ is the basis for our spiritual warfare and the armour is the key to our present salvation being effective. The enemy's fortifications are sustained only by darkness; a misrepresentation of the truth. When the light exposes the lies they will crumble.

The life long, on going process of growing in the realization of God happens one day at a time. As we put on Christ, Who is our righteousness, the old man is put off and we steadily reckon ourselves dead to sin and the world. Being girded with truth and being clothed with Christ's righteousness becomes a life style that equips us to herald the evangel of peace. For most of us, our life, becomes an expression of the living evangel and not that we seek opportunity to herald the good news formally.

## The Helmet and The Sword

*Receive the **helmet of salvation** and the **sword of the spirit,** which is a declaration of God* (Ephesians 6:17).

The verb *to receive,* referring to the helmet and the sword is also in the middle voice. We are not told to put these on.

Neither does God put them on us unawares. We are instructed to **receive** them. It is our privilege to,

**Let the word of Christ dwell in us richly,** *in all wisdom, teaching and admonishing each other, in psalms, and hymns, and spiritual songs, in grace singing in our hearts to the Lord* (Colossians 3:16).

As we let the word dwell in us, God has promised that good things will happen.

*My word which shall fare forth from My mouth. It shall not return to Me empty, but rather, it does that which I desire, and prospers in that for which I sent it* (Isaiah 55:11).

*In the beginning was the word, and the word was toward God,* (John 1:1).

God declared, *"Let light be;"* and light is (Genesis 1:3, Young's Literal). As He was yet speaking the light began to shine. God's spoken word was the power that created the light. The clear declarations of God, to us are also His promises. The fact that He has spoken, we are assured that they are as good as accomplished. To submit our hearts to what He is speaking is to receive the sword of the spirit and to let the word of Christ dwell in us richly. The declarations of Christ are spirit and life (John 6:63). This is His operation, His way of fulfilling all His desire in and through us.

The word of God is still alive and operating (Hebrews 4:12). It now operates in all who receive the sword of the spirit, which is the declarations of Christ. His children that love the truth and receive the sword of the spirit, which is in accord with the evangel of the grace of God will also receive the helmet of salvation one day at a time.

## Be invigorated in the Lord

*For the rest, brethren mine, be invigorated in the Lord and in the might of His strength.* (Ephesians 6:10).

Before we leave this section let us consider the verse leading to the entreaty to *"put on the panoply of God"*. Here we find two key phrases. The first is, **"For the rest"**; in other words, in addition to all I have written in this glorious epistle so far, I am now entreating you to **"be invigorated in the Lord** and **in the might of His strength"**. The elements of the Greek word translated invigorate are "make - IN - ABLE" (Concordant keyword, pg.159). In Christ we are already seated in celestial places and, or among celestial beings. It is in the Lord we need to be invigorated or made able.

To be a saint of God is to be a hallowed one, one set apart for God. We will especially be under attack of the Adversary. The large shield of faith is God's means of protecting ourselves from his onslaught, which is sure to come. It is naïve to think we will be able to quench all his fiery arrows without the shield of faith and it is presumption on our part to think we will be able to stand against his stratagems without God's armour. In Christ, God has graciously provided this wonderful suit of armour. Why would we not take full advantage of it? To receive it and to put it on is our calling and our divine or spiritual service.

## As you Accepted the Lord be Walking in Him

*I am saying this, that no one may be beguiling you with persuasive words. Even if, in flesh, I am absent, nevertheless, in spirit, I am with you, rejoicing and observing your order and the stability of your faith in Christ. **As**, then, **you accepted** Christ Jesus, **the Lord, be walking** in Him* (Colossians 2:4-6).

What joy filled the heart of the apostle Paul as he observed the order and the stability of the faith of the Colossian ecclesia? Their growing realization of God was obvious but this does not stop him from cautioning them to be careful. Apparently there were among them, as there are among us today, those who with persuasive words discount the value of our walk, in the Lord and our behavior.

Paul had heard of this ecclesia's faith in Christ Jesus and the love they had for all saints (1:4). His spirit rejoiced with them. He now exhorts them to continue in the faith. He begins his exhortation with the words "**as you accepted**", or in the same manner that you accepted Christ Jesus, **as your Lord**, now *be walking* in Him (:6), also.

How precious is the fact that God has opened the eyes of our heart to see our desperate need of a Saviour. How thankful we are that He graciously granted us faith to access His saving grace. Nothing can ever impact our lives greater than believing on Christ Jesus but the effect this miracle will have on us daily, is dependent on our continual **walking in the Lord**.

When "Lord" is used as a title of Christ it refers to His authority, and relates to service. (Concordant keyword, pg. 183) To know Him as Lord is to reverence Him as our Master in word and in deed. As His slaves, we eagerly and cheerfully submit to the One Who loves us and gave Himself for us. He has the desire and He has the ability to protect us from all other impostors. Serving Him with our whole heart is freedom indeed, freedom from all other slaveries.

What Paul wrote to Archippus applies to each child of God.

*Look to **the service**, which **you accepted** in the Lord, that you may **be fulfilling it*** (Colossians 4:17).

Nothing can jeopardize our holy calling in Christ or our salvation. These we did not merit or earn. They are wholly in grace, given to us long before we were born.

*God, **saves** us and **calls** us with a holy calling, not in accord with our acts, but **in accord with His own purpose** and the **grace** which is given to us in Christ Jesus before times eonian (2Timothy 1:9).*

*Not for works which are wrought in righteousness which we do, but **according to His mercy, He saves us**, through the bath of renascence and renewal of holy spirit,which He pours out on us richly through Jesus Christ, our Saviour, that, being justified **in** that One's **grace**, we may be becoming enjoyers, in expectation, of the allotment of life eonian (Titus 3:5-7).*

Yet our service is something we fulfill, in the Lord, regardless of how persuasive man's words, of so-called wisdom, are to the contrary. The word "slavery" may bring to mind very negative implications. This is why human wisdom rejects it but it is a lie of the enemy to paint all slavery with the same brush. There is a glorious slavery that is unique from all others. As horrible as it was to be a slave of Sin, the opposite is true, of being a slave to the Lord of Lords and King of Kings. There is no One in a higher position in all creation, to worship, adore and serve. The transcendent greatness of God's power operated in Christ,

*Rousing Him from among the dead and seating Him at His right hand among the celestials, **up over every sovereignty and authority and power and lordship**, and every name that is named, not only in this eon, but also in that which is impending: and subjects all under His feet, and gives Him, as Head over all (Ephesians 1:20-22).*

We are serving a Master, Who has authority over the entire universe. To be associated with Him in any capacity is a high honor. To fully realize we belong to Him is beyond our comprehension. His love poured into our heart enables us to glorify God in all our troubles  as we abide our short time here. He knew how to woo us to Himself and He knows how to care for us. His vast love for us will never fail. As our **rightful Owner**, He will do what is best for us. In fact, He will do above all we can ask for or imagine (Ephesians 3:20).

## Graciously Granting Us All

*Are you not aware that your body is a temple of the holy spirit in you, which you have from God, and you are not your own?  For **you are bought with a price**. By all means glorify God in your body* (1Corinthians 6:19,20).

As slaves of the Lord, it is our joy to glorify God in our body and to do all we do as *work from the soul, as to the Lord and not to men* (Colossians 3:23). However, the evangel of the grace of God is not based on what we must do. It is not a man-centered message at all. It is rather the good news of **what God, through Jesus Christ, has done for us**. Christ crucified is the greatest message possible for all men but it came at the greatest cost to His Father, Who gave up His beloved for us all. We are not able to comprehend the full extent of this cost or the suffering our Lord endured, as He fought the spiritual powers of darkness, with His faith in God as His only weapon.

"This matter of faith creates the stunning coup d'etat [lit. stroke of state – the sudden forcible overthrow of a ruler, Webster's Dictionary] found in the death of Christ on the cross. The final words of Christ came after the three hours of darkness. They were spoken after Christ had been subjected to the terrors of separation from God. They were spoken after the powers of darkness were given free reign. Yet Christ's final words were; "Father into Thy hands am I committing My spirit" (Luke 23:46). . . Christ's faith did not fail. His unfailing faith in the Father is the merit for His resurrection." (Samson as Christ: The Marvelous Opener of the Gates, J. Phillip Scranton, pp. 159,160)

Luke, the beloved physician, records the scene and the words of Jesus the night before His crucifixion, as he knelt in prayer,

*"Father, if it is Thy intention, carry aside this cup from Me. However, **not My will, but Thine,** be done!" Now a messenger from heaven was seen by Him, strengthening Him. And **coming to be in a struggle**, He prayed more earnestly, and His sweat became as if clots of blood descending on the earth* (Luke 22:42-44).

"The Lord well knew the evil that lay ahead of Him, for He had been speaking of it again and again. Moreover, He was well aware of the immeasurable benefits of His death to God, and to all His creation. Does He therefore meet it with stony indifference and stoicism? Are the sufferings less real because they are known and come from God? Not at all! He does not wish to drink the cup. The sufferings of Christ are not His will, but the will of His Father. From the dawn of creation He had delighted in the will of God. He had gladly emptied Himself of the glories of the form of divine and took the form of a slave, and entered into the humiliation of humanity, but when it came to the death of the cross His soul revolted and His will refused to follow. Our wills are instinctively in conflict with God's, so it seems almost impossible for us to realize the awful gulf revealed in the agonizing words, 'not My will, but Thine be done!'" (Concordant Commentary pg. 132, 133)

Realizing the grace in our salvation, and God's love for us, as revealed through His Son's death will cause us to reverently submit as our Lord did to His Father's will in everything, it is our privilege to obey from the heart the One Who **purchased us with His Own blood** (Acts 20:28). We will never regret it.

*Surely, He Who spares not His own Son, but gives Him up for us all, shall together with Him, also, be graciously **granting us all*** (Romans 8:32).

God sacrificed His most precious possession, His Beloved Son. This is now the basis for Him now giving us all else we need. We will never deserve what He has graciously given to us and to attempt to earn it by works of law or by doing anything is to *fall out of grace* (Galatians 5:4).

"Christ's death is representative. When He died, all died potentially. Those who know and believe this glorious fact died with Him to the law, and live with Him unto God. Freedom has dawned. Grace is regnant. Christ is exalted above all. He is enthroned in the hearts of all His saints. His power controls them; His faith is their guiding star; His love, their inspiration and working energy. What need is there for law? None whatever."(Vladimir Gelesnoff, Paul's Epistle to the Galatians p.60)

Christ living in us is our righteousness; rules and rituals and man's self help programs have little attraction. Instead, we sit at His feet and glory in His grace that overwhelms us with faith and love, each day. There is no greater joy than to return His love and walk by His side. According to this world's standards we may be the weak, the ignoble and the contemptible (1Corinthians 1:28) but we are not confused or lost. We have no need for a travel guide or a man-made manual or curriculum to teach us how to serve our Lord.

*For **the saving grace of God** made its advent to all humanity, **training us** that, disowning irreverence and worldly desires, we should be living sanely and justly and devoutly in the current eon, anticipating that happy expectation, even the advent of the glory of the great God and our Saviour Jesus Christ, Who gives Himself for us, that He should be redeeming us from all lawlessness and be cleansing for Himself a people to be about Him, zealous for ideal acts* (Titus 2:11-14).

# CHAPTER 7

## God is After Our Heart

*Now thanks be to God that you were slaves of Sin, yet you **obey from the heart** the type of teaching to which you were given over* (Romans 6:17).

Although, the verse above has been quoted many times it is worthy of even closer consideration. We have attempted to reveal the difference between **obeying from the heart** the clear declarations of Christ, especially Paul's entreaties and striving to be **justified by works of law**. To obey from the heart is to believe God; to take Him at His word and to trust Him. This is an **inward conviction and submission**, that takes place at the very core of our spiritual being, as opposed to an outward toiling.

God has never delighted in rituals or sacrifices (Hebrews 10:8). He has always been after the heart of His children. Obeying from the heart may involve *repentance*, which is primarily the changing of one's mind and a yielding of one's will to His will. The evangel of the grace of God is not a message informing us of what we must do outwardly. It is about God's **inner operation** of the spirit, which alone can change our heart. This principal was prominent in the life and message of Jesus, Himself. One day He was approached by a young man and was asked a sincere question.

*Teacher, what is the great precept in the law? Now He averred to him, "You shall **be loving the Lord your God with your whole heart**, and with your whole soul, and with your whole comprehension. This is the great and foremost precept. Yet the* *second is like it: 'You shall be loving your associate as yourself. On these two precepts is hanging the whole law and the prophets* (Matthew 22:36-40).

To love God with our whole heart is what walking worthily, in the truest sense, is all about. In fact, God's purpose of the eons has always been about winning the hearts of His creatures. Christ's work will be completed when He has conquered every enemy by winning every heart. Then it is said that God will be All in all; He will then be Everything to everybody.

*For Christ must be reigning until He should be placing all His enemies under His feet. The last enemy is being abolished: death. . . . Now, whenever all may be subjected to Him, then the Son Himself also shall be subjected to Him Who subjects all to Him, that **God may be All in all*** (1Corinthians 15:25-28).

## Sin and Righteousness are Conceived in the Heart

In today's society image and political correctness are highly esteemed. Few are open and honest enough to reveal their real self. However, God is not a man; He looks beyond the outward. He is much more concerned with the inner man, *for out of the heart are the issues of life* (Proverbs 4:23, A.V.). Through The Word, not only is God's heart is revealed to us but through His word we get to know our own heart, also.

*The word of God is living and operative, and keen above any two-edged sword, and penetrating up to the parting of soul and spirit, both of the articulations and marrow, and is a judge of the sentiments and **thoughts of the heart**. And there is not a creature, which is not apparent in its sight. Now all is naked and bare to the eyes of Him to Whom we are accountable* (Hebrews 4:12,13).

The heart is the center of our spiritual being and it is the **seat of our motives**. (Concordant Keyword, pg.141) This is why God is after our heart. He needs to get at the root! A heart full of love and affection for its Owner will not stray far.

Jesus taught that sin is conceived in the heart and that it often precedes the outward act itself. He continually made statements like the following that shocked and exposed the hypocrisy of the religious leaders of His time.

*Yet I am saying to you that every man looking at a woman to lust for her already **commits adultery** with her **in his heart*** (Matthew 5:28).

*Not that which is entering into the mouth is contaminating a man, but that which is going out of the mouth; this is contaminating a man* (Matthew 15:11).

*For out of the superabundance **of the heart** the mouth is speaking. The good man out of his good treasure is extracting good things; and the wicked man out of his wicked treasure is extracting wicked things* (Matthew 25:34,35).

"God's way of fullness is that of organic life. In the Divine order life produces its own organism, whether it be vegetable, animal, human, or spiritual. That means that **everything comes from the inside**. Function, order, and fruit issue from this principle of within. Organized Christianity has entirely reversed this order." (T. Austin Sparks, The Stewardship of the Mystery)

So deceptive is **outward appearance** to the soulish man that he is able to convince himself that "image" is virtual reality. From an early age image is the focus and we are taught what is proper and acceptable to **make a good impression**. This is especially true in religious circles, as it also was in Jesus' day, which is evident by His words to the strict Pharisees.

*You Pharisees clean the outside of the cup or plate, while **your secret hearts** are full of greed and selfishness* (Luke 11:39, Weymouth).

The Pharisees knew the law and were good at teaching it to others. Jesus did not have a problem with their teachings and told His followers that they should do all the Pharisee say but don't do what they do for they say one thing and do another (Matthew 23:3). Outwardly they gave the impression that they were keeping the law and some sincerely tried but for the wrong reasons. Their heart was not in it. Righteousness and sin are primarily an issue of the condition and the motives of the heart. Above all else we are to guard our heart (Proverbs 4:23). Whatever is in there will eventually work its way out.

## A Distant Heart

In light of the fact that God is really after our heart, let us explore further God's ultimate purpose to be All in all. Let me suggest that this is primarily a heart issue, also. Once again, the words Jesus spoke to His own people and particularly to the religious leaders of His day, may sound harsh, but are clear and confirm what we are saying.

*Hypocrites! Ideally Isaiah prophesies concerning you, saying, This people with their lips is honoring Me, Yet their **heart is away at a distance** from Me. For out of the heart are coming wicked reasonings, murders, adulteries, prostitutions, thefts, false testimonies, calumnies* (Matthew 15:7,8,19).

We will never **walk worthily**, of the Lord, or **fulfill the just requirement of the law**, as long as our heart is at a distance from our Lord. *God is love* (1John 4:8) and fulfilling the law is only possible through an intimate closeness with Him. It all starts by loving Him with our whole heart; *observing the elements* of the law, in spirit, (Galatians 5:25) will be the natural result. On the other hand also, everything that defiles or causes us to stray off course starts in a heart that has wandered away from the Lord.

All through history are examples of those who experienced a close walk with God, King David being one. Although, he failed miserably at times, yet God said of him *"I found David, of Jesse, **a man according to My heart**, who will be doing all My will"* (Acts 13:22). David learned from his failures by submitting his heart to God and thus grew to cherish God's mercy, grace and his relationship with the Lord above everything else life had to offer. He wrote the following,

*Thy loving kindness is **better than life*** (Psalms 63:3).

*I shall acclaim You, O Yahweh my Elohim, with **all my heart*** (Psalms 86:12).

*With **all my heart**, I have sought after You; I have beseeched Your presence with **all my heart*** (Psalms 119:10,58).

Although, King David had the means to enjoy anything his heart desired, God's loving kindness was the treasure he longed for most. He recognized God as the source of his joy and peace. Christ dwelling in our hearts by faith, basking in His love and our expectation is the one treasure of more value than all else.

*The kingdom of the heavens is like **treasure hidden** in the field, finding which, a man hides it, and, **in his joy**, is going away, and **is selling all**, whatever he has, and is buying that field* (Matthew 13:44).

*The **kingdom of God is** . . . **righteousness** and **peace** and **joy** in holy spirit* (Romans 14:17).

The real treasures in life are not the things we can see and touch; they can't be bought with money but are worth more than anything this world has to offer. The apostle Paul agreed whole-heartedly with King David and Jesus, when he wrote,

*But, to be sure, I am also deeming **all** to be a forfeit because of the superiority of the knowledge of Christ Jesus, my Lord, because of Whom I **forfeited all,** and am deeming it to be refuse, **that I should be gaining Christ** (Philippians 3:8).*

The things of this world that we hold so dear are temporary. Our life is like a vapour, here today, and gone tomorrow. *The fashion of this world is passing by* (1Corinthians 7:31).

*We brought nothing into the world, nor can we carry anything out of it* (1Timothy 6:7, Weymouth).

In today's society one is considered a fool to talk like this but, "He is no fool who gives what he cannot keep to gain what he cannot lose." (Jim Elliot, Through Gates of Splendor, pg.3)

## Wherever Your Treasure is, Your Heart will be also

*Do not hoard for yourselves treasures on earth, where moth and corrosion are causing them to disappear, and where thieves are tunnelling and stealing. Yet hoard for yourselves **treasures in heaven**, where neither moth nor corrosion are causing them to disappear, and where thieves are not tunnelling nor stealing; for **wherever your treasure is, there will your heart be also** (Matthew 6:19-21).*

The idea of depositing and saving in a storehouse somewhere beyond this present earthly existence is a foreign concept to this affluent age that promotes instant gratification. We are not speaking of physical treasures or streets of gold but treasures even more precious and longer lasting. The scriptures are clear; we can "**treasure up**" for the next age; literally, PLACE-INTO-TOMORROW. (Concordant Keyword pg.309) Our apostle Paul used this exact phrase writing to Timothy.

*Be doing good acts, be rich in ideal acts, be liberal contributors, **treasuring up** for yourselves an ideal foundation for that which is impending, that you may get hold of life really* (1Timothy 6:18,19).

Our heart is either treasuring up for this life or the next one, for today or for tomorrow. Can we know where our treasure is? Possibly; ask yourself a few questions. Is the desire of my heart for things that will soon perish? Do I spend the majority of my time and energy attempting to secure a good life here below?

Wherever our treasure is that is where our heart will be also. The irony of this whole issue is in the fact that, being disposed to that which is above, concentrating our desires and energy on treasuring up for the impending age, is God's prescribed way to really get a hold of life now and to enjoy our sojourn here to the fullest. This fact may be unbelievable, even inconceivable and therefore completely hidden to the self-centred soulish man. It is nevertheless in accord with the evangel of God.

## Examining Another's Heart

We are definitely not capable of judging another's hearts on this matter, neither is it our job to do so. We are not even qualified to judge our own heart. However, contrary to the doctrines of some teaching a "pure grace evangel", this does not absolve us in this matter. Instead, we depend on the spirit of God and the light of His word to personally reveal to us where our heart really is and when we stray, also. The Lord Himself, alone can and will reveal to us what we have stored in our innermost caverns, the treasures we are hoarding there, hidden to the natural eye. Paul explained it like this,

*It is the least trifle that I may be being **examined by you** or by man's day. Neither am I **examining myself**. For of nothing am I conscious as to myself, but not by this am I justified. Now **He Who is examining me is the Lord*** (1Corinthians 4:3-4).

The easiest person to fool is ourselves! King David, the man with a pure heart for God is a prime example. God sent Nathan the prophet to David, who told the king a story about two men from the same city; One rich and one poor. The rich had many flocks but the poor man had only one little ewe-lamb, which grew up with him, and with his children. It was like a pet to them. One day a traveler came to the rich man's house and instead of killing one of his many sheep to feed his guest he took the poor man's only lamb and prepared it for the man who had come. When David heard this story his anger burned against the man exceedingly and he said to Nathan, "*surely the man who is doing this must repay fourfold, because he has done this thing, and because that he had no pity*". Nathan said unto David, "*You are the man!*" (2Samuel 12:1-7).

The passage continues by stating how David's conscience was immediately pricked, as  he realized his sin of adultery and murder (:13). The man after God's own heart (Acts 13:22) was deceived until the word of the Lord, through the prophet, opened the eyes of his heart. The same is true for us and for all humans.

One other point of importance is the fact that Nathan went and smote the child that was the result of this adulterous union, with an incurable disease, and the baby died (:15).

The Lord does not examine our hearts because He is unsure what is there, as if it were hidden to Him. *God is greater than our heart, and He knows all* (1John 3:20). He examines our hearts for our benefit. We all have blind spots and much of the time we are not conscious of our faults or the works of the flesh, such as pride and greed motivating us, hindering our walk, and possibly causing others to stumble. We may have been trained well in what is politically and socially correct and are careful to use proper protocol. We may be able to impress the people around us but only God knows what is on the heart.

*Some men's sins are taken **for granted**, preceding them into judging, yet some are **following up** also* (1Timothy 5:24).

A sign of maturity surely must be, to recognize our need for the Lord to examine, judge, and discipline us accordingly, whenever necessary. Nothing will be hidden forever. It would be ideal if all our sins were exposed now and precede us into judgment. The sooner, we face these, and do whatever is in our power to make things right the better, for us and for those we love. The enemy can only work in darkness and secrecy. The grace of God is far greater than our worst sin but keeping things hidden deep in our heart only prolongs the problem and gives it power over us.

God is well aware of all and loves us unconditionally, regardless how severely we miss the mark. We need not fear being disciplined by the Lord. Like all His dealings with us His correction is motivated and tempered by His vast love for us and reaps wonderful rewards immediately and in the future, for all who endure His discipline and are exercised through it.

*Now all discipline, indeed, for the present is not seeming to be a thing of joy, but of sorrow, yet subsequently it is rendering the peaceable fruit of righteousness to those exercised through it* (Hebrews 12:11).

*Being judged, we are being **disciplined by the Lord,** that we may not be condemned with the world* (1Corinthians 11:32).

## Be Testing what is Well Pleasing to the Lord

*All prostitution and uncleanness or greed - let it not even be named among you, according as is becoming in saints - and vileness and stupid speaking or insinuendo, which are not proper, but rather thanksgiving. For this you perceive, knowing that no paramour at all or unclean or greedy person, who is an idolater, has any enjoyment of the allotment in the kingdom of Christ and of God. Let no one be seducing you with empty words, for because of these things the indignation of God is coming on the sons of stubbornness. Do not, then, become joint partakers with them, for you were once darkness, yet now **you are light in the Lord.** As children of light be walking (for the fruit of the light is in all goodness and righteousness and truth), **testing what is well pleasing to the Lord** (Ephesians 5:3-10).*

***Try yourselves,** if you are in the faith; **test yourselves** (2Corinthians 13:5).*

The elements of the Greek word translated "try" is literally PROBIZE and for the word translated "test" is SEEMIZE, which is to form a careful opinion by subjecting the senses or mind to impressions. (Concordant Keyword pp. 300, 311) The verse above was a part of Paul's second letter to Corinth. This is the same ecclesia he had earlier written to informing them that he did not examine himself, because, *"of nothing am I conscious as to myself"* (1Corinthians 4:4). Now he says *"test yourselves".*

Only when the spirit of the Lord examines us, by illuminating His word, are we able to test ourselves properly. It is not that we occupy ourselves with our walk. We live our life freely engaging in what God has given us to do and enjoying our relationship with Him. But because of our deep respect for His word and our reliance on the leading of His spirit, we are naturally and continually forming careful opinions about ourselves. Walking in the light, listening and obeying what the spirit is saying to our heart is an ongoing growing in the realization of God.

*If we should be walking in the light as He is in the light, we are having fellowship with one another* (1John 1:7).

*He who is saying that he is **in the light** and is hating his brother is a liar and is in darkness. He who is loving his brother is remaining in the light* (1John 2:9-10).

All sons of God need discipline. Those who teach otherwise are still in darkness. They are either being seduced by false teachings or they are not sons of God. **Grace does not exempt us** from God's discipline. Grace gives us the endurance and patience with joy to endure it, learn from it and glory in it.

*Discipline are you enduring. As to sons is God bringing it to you, for what son is there whom the father is not disciplining? Now if you are without discipline, of which **all have become partakers**, consequently you are bastards and not sons* (Hebrews 12:7,8).

## Preserve Your Heart

When our heart is disposed to the things of the Lord, it will be drawn to His love and the light of His word. His spirit and His word always agree. We gradually learn to love the truth, especially when it exposes our sin. If we are grieving the spirit or harming a brother we need to know; we want to know. How else can we make amends? We need not fear to see ourselves as we really are. God sees all; He loves us in spite of our faults or else, grace is not grace. God is always near. His love for us never wanes. It  is us who wander away from Him. God will never break fellowship with us but He knows we must deal with the deep realities of life in order to stay close to Him.

The fact remains, wherever our treasure is, our heart is also. If we are not willing to give God our whole heart, religious rituals or hours of study will accomplish little; neither do they  impress God. He wants our whole heart and being. He desires all of us for He is a jealous God (Exodus 34:14). As much as our heart is craving closeness with our Creator He also longs for closeness with us. His love must be returned to be fulfilled.

"The Son of God's love, in Whom we are chosen, is the Firstborn of every creature. There, before all else, God, invisible, imperceptible, created all in the Son of His love. His purpose? His deep, deep yearning? LOVE RESPONSIVE!" (Donald Fielding)

*My son, do attend to my words; To my sayings stretch out your ear; Let them not steal away from before your eyes; **Keep them in** the midst of **your heart**; For they are life to those finding them, And to one's entire flesh, they are health. More than any guard-post, **preserve your heart*** (Proverbs 4:20-23).

Maturity in the Lord does not mean we lose the initial joy of our salvation or our first love for the One Who wooed us to His side. He chose us in Christ before we were born to set us apart for Him alone. It is through our continual acceptance and our enjoyment of this reality that we preserve our heart and find the true purpose for being here in the first place. I must repeat; a revelation of the fact that God handpicked us to be set apart for Him; to worship Him in spirit and in truth will have an enormous impact on our life.

## God Will Judge the Intents of the Heart

We have established the fact that we are not qualified to examine our own heart let alone another's. Based on this understanding some feel there is no place, under any circumstances, to be judging a brother. This seems to be particularly true amongst those who believe in the absolute reign of grace and the eventual reconciliation of all. Verses like the following are used to reinforce this false doctrine.

*Be not judging anything before the season, till the Lord should be coming, Who will also illuminate the hidden things of darkness and manifest the counsels of the hearts. And then applause will be coming to each one from God* (1Corinthians 4:5).

Because it is our heart that God is after and because this is where the issues of life really are it is understandable that He will judge us according to the intents of our heart. Although we are not even to attempt to judge the **hidden things** like the **counsels of the hearts** of others, this is not the whole story. We must see that there is **a difference between judging motives and behavior**. Paul makes it clear that the saints of God can and must judge between themselves on **outward** matters or on **behavior**. We don't concern ourselves with the motive of another's heart. We base our judgment on their actions and then follow the clear-cut instructions given by our apostle.

*Yet now I write to you **not to be commingling** with anyone named a brother, if he should be a paramour, or greedy, or an idolater, or a reviler, or a drunkard, or an extortioner. With such a one you are not even to be eating. For what is it to me to be judging those outside? You are not **judging those within**! Now those outside, God is judging. Expel the wicked one from among yourselves* (1Corinthians 5:11-13).

If and when a brother is conducting himself in a manner that is dishonoring to the Lord and to the evangel, we are exhorted to shun him or expel him from our midst. This may seem harsh but there are times this is the best for the ecclesia, and for that individual. Our instruction when dealing with a sectarian man is, *After one and then a second admonition refuse* (Titus 3:10). We pray for them and leave them with the Lord, for Him to do as He sees fit. When it comes to business matters between brothers we also have clear instructions.

*Dare any of you, having business with another, be judged before the unjust, and not before the saints? Or are you not aware that **the saints shall judge the world**? And if the world is being judged by you, are you unworthy of the least tribunals? Are you not aware that we shall be judging messengers, not to mention life's affairs? If indeed, then, you should have tribunals for life's affairs, the contemptible in the ecclesia, these you are seating? To abash you am I saying this. Thus **is there not among you one wise man who will be able to adjudicate** amidst his brethren, but brother is suing brother, and this before unbelievers!* (1Corinthians 6:1-6).

Paul felt so strongly about this that his goal in writing to the ecclesia at Corinth was to abash or to embarrass them for not dealing with the problem in their midst. He was adamant that those who, in the future, will judge the world and messengers, surely are able to help instruct two brothers how to settle a relatively small dispute. God is the only One qualified to judge the hidden things. **We are exhorted to judge the outward,** *lest the name of God and the teaching may be blasphemed* (1Timothy 6:1).

## Why are you Judging your Brother?

*Let no one be judging you **in food or in drink** or in the particulars of a festival, or of a new moon, or of Sabbaths* (Colossians 2:16).

I realize the whole issue of judging one another is taken too far, especially among the groups that lean toward legalism. Eating and drinking seems to be an area where the enemy can cause havoc. In some circles dress code, make-up, or keeping the Sabbath also are problem issues. As a young believer, attempting to live "the fasting life", judging one another, in our group, was a serious problem, which caused discord and pain.

Paul tells us which brothers to avoid and lists what behavior is unacceptable and to be judged. Issues regarding eating and drinking are not on any of his lists. In response to the legalist's error in going too far in examining each other, the "Pure Grace" advocates err by not going far enough. They tend to overreact to the rules of the "Religious Right" and go to the left too far and misapply the scriptures on this topic. Portions of Romans 14 are often referred to as their guide. They take verses, like those below, referring to eating and drinking etc and apply them carte blanche to any and all areas of behavior. This is gross error!

*Who are you who are judging Another's domestic? To his own Master he is standing or falling* (Romans 14:4)

*Nothing is contaminating of itself, except that the one reckoning anything to be contaminating, to that one it is* (:14).

*All, indeed, is clean, but it is evil to the man who with stumbling is eating* (:20).

*The faith you have, have for yourself in God's sight. Happy is he who is not judging himself in that which he is attesting*

(:22).*Everything which is not out of faith is sin* (:23).

Does lying, stealing or cheating only contaminate those who think it is wrong to do so? What about adultery or murder? Certain behavior is not clean regardless how much faith one believes they have. This is why Paul instructs us to not even eat with anyone who calls himself a brother if he is a paramour (AV fornicator), or greedy, or an idolater, or a reviler, or a drunkard, or an extortioner. We are not to commingle with them (1Corinthians 5:10,11). We are also to avoid a brother who causes dissention (Romans 16:17), and those walking disorderly (2Thessilonians 3:6). Preachers who persist in taking passages dealing with eating and drinking, misapplying them to the more serious conduct that requires strict discipline are false teachers. Following is our instruction when dealing with them.

*If anyone is not obeying our word through this epistle, let it be a sign to you as to this man, **not to commingle** with him, that he may be abashed; and do not deem him as an enemy, but* **admonish him as a brother** (2Thessalonians 3:14,15).

As we stated, Romans 14 is primarily dealing with eating and drinking. This is where we find the phrase used as the subtitle for this section. Let us consider the context of the phrase, which is in the form of a question, "*Why are you judging your brother*" (:10)? By doing so it will not be difficult to see Paul's motive in asking the question.

*Why are you judging your brother? Or why are you also scorning your brother? For all of us shall be presented at the dais of God, for it is written: Living am I, the Lord is saying, For to Me shall bow every knee, And every tongue shall be acclaiming God! Consequently, then, each of us shall be giving account concerning himself to God. By no means, then, should we still be judging one another, rather decide this, **not to place a stumbling block for a brother*** (Romans 14:10-13).

The basic theme of chapter 14 is summarized in the first few verses of the next chapter and is excellent general advice, but especially so, when it comes to the issues of food and drink.

*We, the able, ought to **be bearing the infirmities of the impotent**, (AV weak) and not to be pleasing ourselves. Let each of us please his associate, for his good, toward his edification. For Christ also **pleases not Himself*** (Romans 15:1-3).

The weak are never instructed to bear with the strong, in the faith, but vise versa. It should go without saying, that we do not bear with a brother who is a murderer or an adulterer out of a concern for his edification. Neither should this be our prime motivation when dealing with a brother who is causing division. If the edification of the ecclesia is at stake, the problem must be dealt with because a little leaven will eventually leaven the whole lump (1Corinthians 5:6).

When it comes to personal, private matters such as eating and drinking our main concern is the weaker brother or sister. We do not judge them or do anything to cause them to stumble. As far as facing these issues for ourselves goes; *whatever is not of faith is sin* (Romans 14:13). However, *the faith which you have, have for yourself in God's sight. Happy is he who is not judging himself in that which he is attesting* (:22). The instructions are simple but the context is limited to eating and drinking etc.

*Put on, then as God's chosen ones, holy and beloved, pitiful compassions, kindness, humility, meekness, patience, bearing with one another and **dealing graciously among yourselves**, if anyone should be having a complaint against any. According as the Lord also deals graciously with you, thus also you. Now over all these **put on love**, which is the tie of maturity* (Colossians 3:12-14).

## Salvation and Service

In our ongoing endeavor to *present ourselves to God qualified, an unashamed worker,* we are continually attempting to be *correctly cutting the word of truth* (2Timothy 2:15). To further help us understand the many issues that arise amongst ourselves let us take a closer look at the letters to the ecclesia at Corinth. Here we will see the importance of separating the passages dealing with salvation from the ones dealing with service and then to apply them accordingly. In Paul's first letter to the Corinthians we read,

*I am thanking my God always concerning you over the grace of God which is being given you in Christ Jesus, for in everything are you enriched in him, in all expression and all knowledge, according as the testimony of Christ was confirmed among you, so that you are **not deficient in any grace**, awaiting the unveiling of our Lord Jesus Christ, Who will be confirming you also until the consummation, **unimpeachable** in the day of our Lord Jesus Christ* (1Corinthians 1:4-8).

Paul had established a group of believers in Corinth who had received his evangel. In the first few lines of his first letter to them he thanks God for the grace given to them in Christ Jesus. So great was the testimony of their salvation, that he could say that they were **not deficient in any grace**. They now looked forward to the Lord's return with a great expectation and joy, knowing that God will confirm them **unimpeachable**. They were truly saved in grace through faith and were aware that this was not out of them.

As great as their salvation experience was they had problems. I'm sure Paul would have rather continued writing about the marvelous work of grace in their midst but instead he is quickly compelled to bring up the topic of their service.

*I, brethren, could not speak to you as to spiritual, but as to fleshy, as to minors in Christ. Milk I give you to drink, not solid food, for not as yet were you able. Nay, still, not even now are you able, for **you are still fleshly**. For where there is **jealousy** and **strife** among you, are you not fleshly and walking according to man* (1Corinthians 3:1-3)?

Although their salvation was secure they were minors, walking in accord with the flesh. Brothers were suing each other; they were having lawsuits amongst themselves, injuring and cheating one another (6:6-8). Besides these issues, prostitution was also a serious problem in this ecclesia. Paul speaks more about this particular sin to those in Corinth than in all his other letters. Below are a few of the references made to prostitution.

*Absolutely, it is heard that there is prostitution among you, and such prostitution (which is not even named among the nations), so that someone has his father's wife* (5:1).

*The body is not for prostitution, but for the Lord, and the Lord for the body* (6:13).

***Flee from prostitution****. The penalty of every sin, whatsoever a man should be doing, is outside of the body, yet he who is committing prostitution is sinning against his own body* (6:18).

*Nor yet may we be committing prostitution* (10:8).

In his second letter Paul refers again to the same issue, which had not been dealt with sufficiently. He warns them that when he comes again this issue will have to be dealt with.

*Not again at my coming will my God be humbling me toward you, and **I shall be mourning for many** who have sinned before and are **not repenting** of the uncleanness and prostitution and wantonness which they commit* (2Corinthians 12:21).

I say all this, to make two important points. First to show that even such a serious sin as prostitution does not cancel God's saving grace. When it came to God's choice and calling and their salvation they were **not deficient in any grace**. The second point is; even though prostitution was an obvious problem amongst them that must be dealt with, he does not single out this sin to expose them as still being fleshly.

Their **jealousy and the strife** was the **telltale sign** of their immaturity. This subject we will discuss in more detail later. For now let us look at the importance of distinguishing between our salvation in grace and our service in the Lord. There is a world of difference between the favor God has bestowed on us in Christ, and the rewards He hands out. One is a gift the other is a wage. In chapter three of the first letter to the Corinthians we read ,

*Now he who is planting and he who is irrigating are for one thing. Yet **each will be getting his own wages according to his own toil.** For God's fellow workers are we. God's farm, God's building, are you. (1 Corinthians 3:8,9).*

Once we realize the grace of God in truth; we become a new creation in Christ; we are eligible to be God's fellow workers and receive wages according to the kind of work we perform.

*Each one's work will become apparent, for the day will make it evident, for it is being revealed by fire. And the fire, it will be **testing each one's work** - what kind it is. If anyone's work will be remaining which he builds on it, **he will get wages.** If anyone's work shall be burned up, he will forfeit it, yet he shall be saved, yet thus, as through fire. Are you not aware that you are a temple of God and the spirit of God is making its home in you? If anyone is corrupting the temple of God, God will be corrupting him, for the temple of God is holy, which you are (:13-17).*

The work we perform, while on earth, will be tested by fire. If anyone's work does not stand the test and is all burned up, it is written, *"He will forfeit it."* What will he forfeit? The verse before clearly tells us: it is his wages. He will not get wages, *yet he shall be saved yet thus, as through fire.* (:15).

To be unimpeachable in the day of our Lord Jesus Christ does not guarantee wages for our labor, in the Lord. The fire will consume all unworthy work yet the believer himself will be saved. God has made His home in us and in that respect we are eternally secure but we may still suffer great loss in that day when the Lord comes.

*Who will also illuminate the hidden things of darkness and manifest the counsels of the hearts. And then applause will be coming to each one from God* (1Corinthians 4:5).

We are sure the apostle Paul was not speaking about losing our salvation but we must notice to what lengths he writes about receiving a reward for service. Also, in this first letter to Corinth he compares serving the Lord to competing in the Grecian games of that time.

*Now all am I doing because of the evangel, that I may be becoming a joint participant of it. Are you not aware that those racing in a stadium are, indeed, all racing, yet one is obtaining the prize? Thus be racing that you may be grasping it. Now every contender is controlling himself in all things; they, indeed, then, that they may be obtaining a corruptible wreath, yet we an incorruptible. Now then, thus am I racing, not as dubious, thus am I boxing, not as punching the air, but I am belaboring my body and leading it into slavery, lest somehow, when heralding to others, I myself may become disqualified* (1Corinthians 9:23-27).

Paul's motivation for all he did was the furtherance of the evangel. He makes it clear he is not participating in the race just for the fun of it. Neither was he shadow boxing. The race and the fight he was involved in, are real and the prize to those who run faithfully, according to the rules, is also real. He was willing to belabor or buffet his body, even to lead it into slavery to ensure that he would not be disqualified. The reward he is anticipating, when he stands before the dais of Christ, is an incorruptible wreath. Although it has nothing to do with salvation the reality and the glory of it caused him to forsake all other contests in order to obtain this one prize.

*Wherefore we are ambitious . . . to be well pleasing to Him. For all of us must be manifested in front of the dais of Christ, that each should be requited for that which he puts into practice through the body, whether good or bad. Being aware, then, of the fear of the Lord, we are persuading men, yet we are manifest to God* (2Corinthians 5:9-11).

## Severed for the Evangel of God

Paul was *a slave of Christ Jesus, a called apostle, **severed for the evangel of God*** (Romans 1:1), *the evangel of the glory of the happy God* (1Timothy 1:11,12). He did not choose this calling and although he only became aware of it on the Damascus road, he later realized that,

**God severs me from my mother's womb** *and calls me through His grace, to unveil His Son in me that I may be evangelizing Him among the nations* (Galatians 1:15,16).

The apostle Paul was also entrusted with ushering in a new administration, which is "an orderly arrangement for the management of affairs." (Concordant Keyword pg.10)

The inspired title for God's new arrangement, during this period in history, is called "**The administration of the grace of God**". A primary purpose of this writing is to shed light, however dimly, on how God is managing His affairs with mankind and especially with believers, at this time. There seems to be so much confusion amongst some believers regarding this administration and so little interest in others.

*Surely you hear of the administration* (dispensation A.V.) *of the grace of God that is given to me* [Paul] *for you, for by revelation the secret is made known to me* (Ephesians 3:2,3).

The grace of our Lord overwhelmed Paul *with faith and love in Christ Jesus.* His testimony was this, *"that Christ Jesus came into the world to save sinners, foremost of whom am I. But therefore was I shown mercy, that in me, the foremost, Jesus Christ should be displaying all His patience, for a **pattern of those who are about to be believing** on Him for life eonian"* (1Timothy 1:14-16).

The **foremost sinner** was chosen to be a display of all God's patience. As such, he became God's ideal candidate to be the **pattern** or prototype of those who are about to believe under this new arrangement called the administration of the grace of God.

Although Paul was a member of the chosen Jewish nation he was appointed to take the evangel to the nations who were not, as a whole, actively zealous for God as were the Jews. Paul quotes the prophetic word of Isaiah (65:1) to further reveal the nature of this administration and of grace itself.

*I was found by those who are not seeking Me; I became disclosed to those who are not inquiring for Me* (Romans 10:20).

## Christ Among Us

Paul was more than a pattern believer in the new arrangement. He was also the dispenser of the evangel of God (Colossians 1:23) and was given many glorious revelations. He refers to one in particular, "**Christ among you**", that we must focus on.

*I became a dispenser, in accord with the administration of God, which is granted to me for you, to **complete the word of God - the secret** which has been concealed from the eons and from the generations, yet now was made manifest to His saints to whom God wills to make known what are the glorious riches of this secret among the nations, which is: **Christ among you**, the expectation of glory (25-27).*

Notice the two connected phrases referring directly to the revelation of Christ among us. Paul stated it was given to him **to complete the word of God - the secret.**

The revelation of Christ among us, the nations was a secret previously hid, waiting for the right time to be revealed. It now becomes a focal point of the new administration of the grace of God; so much so that it is necessary to complete the inspired, written word of God, for the body of Christ, for today.

Let me suggest, this secret not only represents the **uniqueness** but also the **climax** of Paul's ministry and this glorious dispensation. Therefore, it must epitomize what the eyes of our heart are longing to behold. However, we are not just speaking of a mere mental assent to a doctrine. Comprehending the significance of the secret of Christ among us should have a dynamic impact on us as a body. Firstly, we must realize that there is a deeper aspect to completing the word of God than simply to be unveiling a secret.

Our goal is not to diminish the fact that this is a glorious truth. We, also readily admit that we can only perceive the importance of it, on any level, because of the riches of His grace. But to be content, to merely sit back, and glory in the fact that we are now **the enlightened ones**, is to stop on the far side of Jordan, and never enter into **our Canaan land**, so to speak.

There must be a deeper level, on which the body of Christ will experience "Christ among you", before we meet the Lord in the air. The apathy, indifference and strife among us, all testify to the fact that the eyes of our hearts have not really been enlightened yet, to perceive the glory of His allotment among the saints (Ephesians 1:18). When our hearts grasp the transcendent greatness of His power for us who are believing (:19) then it must be that the word of God will be completed **practically** or **experientially** and Christ among us will not just be a doctrine but **a living, operating reality**.


## Christ is Completing All

*He Who descends is the Same Who ascends also, up over all who are of the heavens, that He should be **completing all*** (Ephesians 4:10).

God has had one **specific end in mind** each time He chose and called an apostle, prophet, evangelist, pastor or teacher since the beginning of the body of Christ's long history. To this end He has been slowly but surely moving toward all along.

*Toward the adjusting of the saints for the work of dispensing, for the upbuilding of the body of Christ **unto the end** that we should **all attain** to the **unity of the faith** and of the realization of the son of God, to a **mature man**, to the measure of the stature of the **complement of the Christ** (:11-13).*

The day is coming come when **the earth shall be filled with the knowledge of God's glory**, *as the waters cover the sea* (Habakkuk 2:14). The whole creation has an intuitive feeling or sense that something cataclysmic is going to happen that will end the global bondage to decay and mortality.

*For the premonition of the creation is awaiting the unveiling of the sons of God that the creation itself, also, shall be freed from* **the slavery of corruption** *into the glorious freedom of the children of God. For we are aware that the entire creation is groaning and travailing together until now. Yet not only so, but we ourselves also, who have the firstfruit of the spirit, we ourselves also, are groaning in ourselves, awaiting the sonship,* **the deliverance of our body** (Romans 8:19-23).

This fatal event is in accord with **the unveiling of the sons of God**. Even now, we are the first to be God's temple or the habitation of the living God on earth. Christ is the spirit that has taken its abode in us. We are *sealed with the holy spirit of promise which is an earnest of the enjoyment of our allotment* (Ephesians 1:13,14). Christ in us is our guarantee that full deliverance is coming  for us and also for the whole creation. We are chosen to play an integral part in liberating the universe.

Understandably, it is difficult for us to comprehend how we can accomplish anything towards this end until after we are with the Lord in our glorified bodies. The fact remains, that Christ has taken His abode in each and every member of His body, and He has begun a mighty operation of the spirit **among us**, even now. Grasping this secret must be a key to bringing us all to maturity.

The foundation has been laid; the preparation for us to be *the complement of the One completing the all in all* (:23) has already begun.

As Jesus once walked the earth and dwelt in the land of Israel He now, in spirit walks among us preparing us for our future allotment when *in the oncoming eons, He should be displaying the transcendent riches of His grace in His kindness to us in Christ Jesus* (Ephesians 2:7).

Before the foundation of the world we were chosen for this purpose. Our preliminary training, during our sojourn on earth, is a necessary step to equip us to serve in the celestials. This is **the primary purpose** of our short existence here and the basis for our spiritual warfare, also. The enemy will do all he can to separate us and distract us from daily growing in the realization of God's will and the main reason why we were born, chosen, called and set apart, in the first place.

Many saints feel that "unity of the faith" means agreeing on doctrine and understanding all the same revelations and that this is necessary to prepare us for our future allotment. I am not so sure. It seems unlikely that all believers will ever see eye to eye on the great truths we glory in. Could this theory be a deception of the enemy to cause the saints of God to waste much time and energy debating doctrine? Could it be to distract from the real meaning and pursuit of the unity of the faith?

## Presenting Every Man Mature

As the beloved John reclined at dinner he leaned back on the chest of Jesus (John 21:20). We also, in spirit, can have an intimate relationship with our Lord and Saviour. The glorified Son of God, Who Paul met on the Damascus Road and then preached is the Christ among us. The unity of the faith must be based on our closeness or oneness with Him. Christ among us is our *expectation of glory* (Colossians 1:27). Paul toiled and struggled to the end of his days to make this secret known.

*Whom we are announcing, admonishing every man and teaching every man in all wisdom, that we should be presenting **every man mature** in Christ Jesus for which **I am toiling also, struggling in accord with His operation,** which is operating in me with power* (:28,29).

The apostle's goal in heralding Christ was to present all mature in Christ. The opposition to the operation of God's power in him was ever present as he struggled, through incredible trials and persecution, to announce the good news, to teach and admonish all who would listen. He often stood alone and makes a special mention of the few who **struggled with him.** Near the end of his letter to the Colossians he wrote,

*Greeting you is Epaphras, who is one of you, a slave of Christ Jesus, always struggling for you in prayers, that you may **stand mature** and fully assured in all the will of God* (Colossians 4:12).

If our heart's desire is to share God's evangel, and the secret, of Christ among us, we can expect a struggle as well. The opposition against us is not a sign of God's displeasure but to the contrary. It may be a sign of the enemy's tactics to discourage us but ultimately, it is a necessary part of God's intention for us, so that we learn to grow in the realization of Him. God's message to all with ears to hear is this,

*I want you to perceive what the struggle amounts to which I (Paul) am having for your sakes that your **hearts may be consoled**, being **united in love**, and to all the riches of the assurance of understanding, unto **a realization of the secret** of the God and Father, of Christ* (Colossians 2:1,2).

A growing realization of Christ among us will undoubtedly cause us a struggle. There will be opposition from without and from within, from legalists and fatalists. If we, the saints, can **perceive what the struggle amounts to,** our hearts will be consoled, we will be *united in love* (:1) and will gain all the *riches of the assurance of understanding* even *unto a realization of the secret* (:2). But we must be careful. Paul went on to caution us.

*I am saying this, that **no one may be beguiling you** with persuasive words. For even if, in flesh, I am absent, nevertheless, in spirit, I am with you, rejoicing and observing your order and the stability of your faith in Christ. As, then, you accepted Christ Jesus, the Lord, be walking in Him* (:4-6).

Some of our opposition will come in the form of an attack of false teachings, persuasive words to destroy our stability and even our faith in Christ and the evangel of God. What is the answer to guard against and to deal with this onslaught of the enemy. It is simply to continue to **be walking in Him** (:6), *having been rooted and being built up in Him* (:7).

We must beware that no one ruins, or seizes what we have already attained in Christ, *through philosophy and empty seduction, in accord with human tradition and the elements of the world and not in accord with Christ* (:8).

*In Christ the entire complement of the Deity is dwelling bodily. And you are complete in Him* (:9,10).

Paul goes on and exposes the vanity of the legalist's traditions and rituals, ceremonies and decrees (:16-23). He then attacks the false notions of the fatalist who carries absolute truth that we are complete in Christ too far. Lest we become apathetic and indifferent and fall asleep in our daily walk, Paul continues in Colossians chapter 3 with these words.

*If, then, you were roused together with Christ, **be seeking that which is above**, where Christ is, sitting at the right hand of God. **Be disposed to that which is above**, not to that on the earth, for you died, and your life is hid together with Christ in God*

(Colossians 3:1-3). **Deaden, then, your members** *that are on the earth: prostitution, uncleanness, passion, evil desire and greed, which is idolatry* (:5).

*Now you also be* **putting away all these**: *anger, fury, malice, calumny, obscenity out of your mouth. Do no lie to one another, stripping off the old humanity together with its practices, and* **putting on the young**, *which is being renewed into recognition, to accord with the Image of the One Who creates it* (:8-10).

The secret of Christ among us and our completeness in Him is in accord with the evangel, which is God's power for salvation. Our salvation is a relationship with our glorified Lord. Christ is our righteousness. We are complete in Him. Therefore, as we accepted Him let us continue to keep walking in Him, in spirit, daily rejoicing together, in the stability of our faith.

## The One Body is Christ's Complement

God gives Christ, *as Head over all, to the ecclesia which is His body,* **the complement of the One completing the all in all** (Ephesians 1:23).

Complement is that which fills. (Concordant Keyword pg. 108) It remains a mystery to many, who name the name of the Lord, that the body is to complete the Head. It may be difficult for us, at this time, to even consider how it is possible to be a part of that which fills or completes Christ. How could the One, Who is above every sovereignty and authority and power and lordship need anything from you and me to be complete?

If it is possible that the body is necessary to complete the Head, and it must be, there is one critical aspect we must see regarding this truth. **God gave Christ** as Head over all **to the**

**ecclesia** His body. Therefore, each of us must become subject to the Head; this is how we become one together. This is how we discover our unity in Christ. One member or **divided members cannot be His complemen**t. His unified body is His complement.

It is not too difficult to imagine why we will be unified in our future allotment, no longer hindered by mortality. Then we will operate in complete harmony, doing God's perfect will, together, each one subject to the Head. What may be more difficult for us to realize is that we are also, **now being prepared**, for our celestial calling, **together**. Christ is operating among us, as a body, now although we are isolated in more ways than one.

Notice, in the verses preceding the truth about the body being Christ's complement, how many times the pronoun "**us**" is used, referring to Christ's **one body**.

*God blesses **us** with every spiritual blessing among the celestials, in Christ, according as He chooses **us** in Him before the disruption of the world, we to be holy and flawless in His sight, in love designating **us** beforehand for the place of a son for Him through Christ Jesus; in accord with the delight of His will, for the laud of the glory of His grace, which graces **us** in the Beloved: in Whom **we** are having the deliverance through His blood, the forgiveness of offenses in accord with the riches of His grace, which He lavishes on **us**; in all wisdom and prudence making known to **us** the secret of His will (in accord with His delight, which He purposed in Him) to have an administration of the complement of the eras, to head up all in the Christ - both that in the heavens and that on the earth (Ephesians 1:3-10).*

We are members of one another, **blessed together, chosen together** and **designated together.** God lavishes His grace **on us** and makes known the secret of His will **to us,** as a body. Christ's allotment is **among** the saints. The operation of His might and strength is given to "us" **as a body.** It does not only operate in individuals but in very real way it operates between us.

A big part of our training to prepare us to be useful in the future has to do with relating to one another now. Now is the time for us to learn how to support, pray and to submit to one another in love, if we are to be useful later.

*With humility, deeming one another superior to one's self* (Philippians 2:3)

*With all humility and meekness, with patience, **bearing with one another** in love . . . being **subject to one another** in the fear of Christ* (Ephesians 4:2, 5:21).

*Through love be **slaving for one another*** (Galatians 5:13).

*The entire building, being **connected together**, is growing into a holy temple in the Lord: in Whom you, also, are being **built together** for God's dwelling place, in spirit* (Ephesians 2:21,22).

*Now, being true, in love we should be **making all grow into Him, Who is the Head** – Christ* (Ephesians 4:15).

We who are connected in the Lord are being built together for God's dwelling place in spirit. It is impossible to be one with the Lord and not with each other. We are all one; as the Father is in Christ, and Christ is in the Father we also are one together in Them (John 17:21). The glory that the Father gave Christ, He gives to us that we may be one, according as They are One (:22).

*For we, **who** are many, **are one body in Christ**, yet individually members of one another* (Romans 12:5).

*For even as the body is one and has many members, yet all the members of the one body, being many, are **one body**, thus also is the Christ. For **in one spirit** also we all are baptized into **one body*** (1Corinthians 12:12,13).

*God **blends the body together**, giving to that which is deficient more exceeding honour, that there may be **no schism in the body*** (:24,25).

## Striving For Unity

*I am entreating you, then, I, the prisoner in the Lord, to **walk worthily** of the calling with which you were called, with all humility and meekness, with patience, bearing with one another in love, endeavouring to **keep the unity** of the spirit with the tie of peace: **one** body and **one** spirit, according as you were called also with **one** expectation of your calling; **one** Lord, **one** faith, **one** baptism, **one** God and Father of all, Who is over all and through all and in all.  And the same One gives these, indeed, as apostles, yet these as prophets, yet these as evangelists, yet these as pastors and teachers, toward the adjusting of the saints for the work of dispensing, for the upbuilding **of the body** of Christ, unto the end that we should **all attain to the unity** of the faith and of the realization of the son of God, to a mature man, to the measure of the stature of the complement of the Christ, that we may by no means still be minors, surging hither and thither and being carried about by every wind of teaching, by human caprice, by craftiness with a view to the systematizing of the deception. Now, being true, in love we should be making **all*** *grow into Him, Who is the Head – Christ out of Whom the **entire body**, being articulated together and **united** through every assimilation of the supply, in accord with the operation in measure of each one's part, is making for the growth of the body, for the upbuilding of itself in love* (Ephesians 4:1-16).

Bearing with each other in love is a sign of maturity. In the spirit there is unity. Strife is a sure sign of walking according to flesh. All God's gifts and callings are given by the spirit with one end in mind; that we **all attain to the unity of the faith,** to build up the body of Christ. Together, we must grow in the realization of the son of God, to the measure of the stature of the complement of the Christ. The **entire body,** is being **built together** and **united through** the supply of **each one's part.**

Those who believe only a handful of evangelists and teachers are responsible for the growth of the body are conceited and sadly misinformed. Worse yet, a sectarian spirit is motivating them, albeit unawares. Leaders and followers must guard against this deception. Only as we are subject to Christ, our Head, can we realize our need for all members of the body.

## The Expectation Reserved for Us in the Heavens

*We are thanking the God and Father of our Lord Jesus Christ, always praying concerning you, on hearing of your faith in Christ Jesus and the love which you have for all the saints, because of the expectation reserved for you in the heavens which you hear before in the word of truth of the evangel* (Colossians 1:3-5).

Notice the hinge-word "because". It joins two critical thoughts. On one side of the hinge is our **faith in Christ** and **our love for all saints.** These two vital elements hang and swing on the reality of our **expectation in the heavens**. Our love for all saints and our faith in Christ is because of our expectation to be together as a body with Christ in the heavens.

*Our realm is inherent in the heavens* (Philippians 3:20).

The elements of the Greek for the word translated *inherent* or belong is UNDER-ORIGINATE , it is used of a permanent actual possession. (Concordant Keyword pg. 30) There is a permanent allotment for the body of Christ, in the heavens. It is Christ's allotment, as the Head but is reserved for the whole body, the Head and all the members subject to the Head.

It is our connection to Christ that joins us together and makes us members of one another. If we have a sectarian expectation it will reflect on our lack of love for all saints and may possibly be a sign of feigned faith.

"Our expectation is one of the most powerful things to consider because of the effect that it has upon our life if we get a glimpse of it. A vague and abstract concept of the here after will have little effect on our lives." (A. E. Knoch, Unsearchable Riches, vol.63)

It would be almost comical if it was not such a sad fact that there are those in isolated little groups and sects who scoff at Christendom for its juvenile perception of the hereafter. They can readily see the mote in their brother's eye and are clueless to the beam in their own (Matthew 7:3). They have been duped into believing that the reason they can have fellowship with so few others, is because they have a superior revelation of their calling and heavenly allotment.

When I was a youth, growing up in a Mennonite church I heard a joke about a person who died and was met by Saint Peter at the pearly gates to receive a tour of heaven. As they approached a closed door, Peter put his finger to his lips and said, "hush, this a room full of Baptists and they think they are the only ones here". At that time I thought it was very funny. What is really funny, if I may use that word loosely, is the fact that almost every group has a similar mentality. Some leaders even teach their followers that the deeper the revelation of God and His ways, the smaller the group will be, therefore those with the most light are the most sectarian. I am not suggesting anyone join a denominational church. I am only making the point that we may be susceptible to a sectarian spirit, which is in direct opposition to the revelation of "Christ among you".

The expectation reserved in the heavens is for all the saints together as one body, regardless of how few or how many there will be. This fact is in accord with the truth of the evangel of the grace of God. When the message of the grace of our Lord overwhelms us, it will be with faith and love in Christ Jesus (1Timothy 1:14). This love will be not only for Christ the Head but for all members of the body, who are one with Him, also.

## Love is the Key to Understanding

*To be made staunch with power, through His spirit, in the man within, Christ to dwell in your hearts through faith, that you, having been **rooted and grounded in love,** should be strong to grasp, together with **all the saints**, what is the breadth and length and depth and height* (Ephesians 3:16-18).

Spiritual truth cannot be learned, it must be revealed by the spirit, to the eyes of the heart. By being grounded in love our hearts are made strong to grasp the deep things of God; things beyond the mind's comprehension. Our goal is,

*To know the love of Christ as well which transcends knowledge - that we may be completed for the entire complement of God* (Ephesians 3:19).

*Now, being true, in love we should be making all grow into Him, Who is the Head - Christ* (Ephesians 4:15).

Love can take our hearts to heights and depths of spiritual understanding that transcends the knowledge of our minds. Love is the only thing that can bring unity among the saints, for *Love is the tie of maturity* (Colossians 3:14).

## Holding the Head

"Holding the Head' is a succinct [right to the point] expression of our duty as members of the body of Christ. A conscious connection to Him as our Head will sever us from the things of the world, whether it be its religion (however divine its origin) or its philosophy. Any attempt to improve our position before God by physical means, whether it be an appeal to the senses or a curbing of its normal needs, denies our completeness in Christ". (Concordant Commentary pg. 305)

*The husband is head of the wife even as **Christ is Head of the ecclesia**, and He is the Saviour of the body. Nevertheless, as **the ecclesia is subject to Christ**, thus are the wives also to their husbands **in everything*** (Ephesians 5:23,24).

*He (Christ) is before all, and all has its cohesion in Him. And **He is the Head of the body, the ecclesia**, Who is Sovereign, Firstborn from among the dead* (Colossians 1:18).

Our glory as members in Christ's body first and foremost is in being subject to the Head. A continual conscious connection to

Him will not only sever us from the things of this world but will instill a love in us for all who are His. Christ is Head. We as His body are complete as we abide in Him. As individual members we are, in a practical way only complete together, as His body subject to the Head.

*Being **entombed together** with Him in baptism, in Whom you were **roused together** also through faith in the operation of God, Who rouses Him from among the dead, you also being dead to the offenses and the uncircumcision of your flesh, He **vivifies us together** jointly with Him* (Colossians 2:12,13).

"The divine picture of our portion is the physical body of Christ, risen and ascended and seated at God's right hand in the celestial spheres. As the physical members are to this body, so we, His spiritual members, are to Him. We too, are roused and seated there, and are the instruments through which He will effect His Father's will in the empyrean [celestial realm]." (Concordant Commentary pg. 305)

Christ among us is our expectation of glory (Colossians 1:27). By **holding the Head,** out of Whom **the entire body,** being supplied and united through the assimilation and ligaments, **is growing in the growth of God** (:19).

The supply of what the whole body needs to sustain itself, and to maintain its unity, comes from Christ our Head. But the entire body is being supplied and united through the figurative ligaments that connect us and hold the different parts of the body together. When the body is not subject to the Head in everything it loses the reality of its completeness in Christ. When its members let go of their hold of Christ they lose their connection with the other members of the body and therefore to the vital supply that sustains growth.

# CHAPTER 8

## Amazing Grace

### Glorified Together with The Lord

*Yet if children, enjoyers also of an allotment, enjoyers, indeed, of an allotment from God, yet joint enjoyers of Christ's allotment, if so be that we are suffering together, that we should be glorified together also* (Romans 8:17).

*The dead in Christ shall be rising first, then we who are living, who are remaining over, together with them shall be caught away in clouds to meet the Lord in air, and so always with the Lord we shall be; so, then, comfort one another in these words* (1Thessalonians 4:16-18, Young's Literal).

In this life all God's children **suffer and wait together**, longing for the day we will be **changed together** into the likeness of Christ's glory. **Together** also, we will be **caught away** to meet the Lord in the air; and we shall **always be together** with Him. How can anything be more comforting to us in these wicked days then the living reality of our great expectation in Christ?

*If we are having an expectation in Christ in this life only, more forlorn than all men are we (Yet now Christ has been roused from among the dead, the Firstfruit of those who are reposing . . . yet **we all shall be changed** in an instant, in the twinkle of an eye, at the last trump. For He will be trumpeting, and the dead will be roused incorruptible, and we shall be changed* (1Corinthians 15:19,20,52).

## Reigning Together

*I am enduring all because of those who are chosen, that they also may be happening upon the salvation, which is in Christ Jesus with glory eonian. Faithful is the saying: "For if we died together, we shall be living together also; **if we are enduring, we shall be reigning together also**; if we are disowning, He also will be disowning us; if we are disbelieving, He is remaining faithful - He cannot disown Himself* (2Timothy 2:10-13).

The above passage, was written near the end of Paul's life; probably in the last book he wrote. Here he stated that all he endured, which was plenty, is for the sake of those chosen, that they would be saved and enjoy God's glory for the eons. He follows with, what he calls, a faithful saying that has caused God's people much concern and debate. He begins by stating that **if we died** with Christ **we will** also **be living** together with Him. The word "if" does not express any doubt in his mind. He is simply repeating a fact that he had previously established.

*__If we died__ together with Christ, we believe that **we shall be living together** with Him also* (Romans 6:8).

*The love of Christ is constraining us, judging this that if One died for the sake of all, consequently **all died*** (2Corinthians 5:14).

*Be disposed to that which is above, not to that on the earth, **for you died**, and your life is hid together with Christ in God* (Colossians 3:2,3).

*Are you ignorant that whoever are baptized into Christ Jesus, are **baptized into His death*** (Romans 6:3)?

The fact is clear; all who died with Christ shall be **living with Him**, also. This will eventually be true for all mankind, also.

*Even as, in Adam, all are dying, thus also, in Christ, shall all be vivified. Yet each in his own class* (1Corinthians 15:22,23).

To be vivified is to be given life beyond the reach of death. (Concordant Keyword, pg. 320)

Let us consider the second part of the faithful saying, from 2Timothy 2, which, I presume has been the cause of even more discussion than the first, *if we are **enduring**, we shall be **reigning together** also; if we are disowning, He also will be disowning us* (:12). We are sure, Paul is not contradicting what he just said about our assurance of being with Christ. He has moved on from speaking about being saved in grace and is now talking about something greater than living with Christ; that is reigning with Him. **Those who endure will reign.** Endurance has to do with faithfulness in service. Only those who endure now will reign later!

"Endurance will be recognized by a place of authority in His celestial realm. If we disown Him we cannot expect Him to give us a public place of power in the future. This does not infringe in the least degree on our salvation or life or anything, which is ours by His grace." (Concordant Commentary, pg. 325)

Regardless of what position we will hold in the celestial realm, we will be together with the Lord for a long, long time. How can this revelation not stir up a love for each member of Christ's body and an awareness of our need for unity?

## Competing Together in the Faith of the Evangel

Paul's letter to the Philippians is written to **all saints in Christ Jesus** (Philippians 1:1) who are *joint participants of grace* (:7). To all believers, one primary entreaty or charge is given,

*Only be citizens walking worthily of the evangel of Christ . . .*
*standing firm in one spirit, one soul, **competing together** in the*
*faith of the evangel* (Philippians 1:27).

It is a curious matter that we who claim to be the *administrators*
*of God's secrets* (1Corinthians 4:1), and the *ambassadors of God*
(2Corinthians 5:20) appear to have little concept of what it is to
be *competing together for the evangel.* The first century church
did not have the completed written word of God but they had a
zeal in the faith that puts us to shame. They knew nothing of
the great revelations of Paul's prison epistles yet the simple
message of Christ crucified filled their hearts with joy and
quickly spread and flourished. We are told that,

*They were persevering in the teaching of the apostles, and in*
*fellowship, and in the breaking of bread, and in prayers . . . Now*
*all those who believe also were in the same place and had all*
*things in common . . . Besides **persevering day by day with one***
***accord** in the sanctuary, besides breaking bread home by home,*
*they partook of nourishment with exultation and simplicity of*
*heart, praising God and having favor for the whole people. Now*
*the Lord added those being saved day by day*
(Acts 2:42-47).

*They spoke the word of God with boldness. Now the multitude*
*of those who believe were of **one heart and soul,** and not even*
*one said that any of his possessions are his own, but it was all*
*theirs in common. And with great power the apostles rendered*
*testimony to the resurrection of Jesus Christ, the Lord. Besides,*
*great grace was on them all* (4:31-33).

Here we have a picture of a people who understood what it
means to **compete together for the evangel**. It seems obvious
that the joy of their salvation and sharing the good news was
their **main priority in life**. They not only spent much time

together talking about it but they prayed together and gave generously and cheerfully to support the heralding of the message. The apostles of that day were free to *be persevering in prayer and the dispensation of the word* (Acts 6:4).

In contrast to this scenario, many saints, at least in this western, affluent part of the world, seem to be void of this vision and therefore a zeal in this regard. Many are content to live their life in relative luxury, doing their own thing and pursuing their own goals, year after year. Supporting the "work of the Lord", is reduced to attending church once a week or a few conferences a year. Some pay their tithes, others drop a few dollars in the collection plate and pay for a subscription to receive a magazine from those laboring in the word. This fulfills their commitment to ensure the spreading of the word.

However, much time, energy and finances can be spent every year on planning and enjoying exotic holidays while the good news sits on the bookshelf collecting dust. I realize this is not a popular topic but we must not ignore the passages written on it because they are unpopular. The same apostle who shared the revelations about the grace of God wrote much about the giving of our time, energy and finances, also.

*He who is sowing sparingly, sparingly shall be reaping also, and who is **sowing bountifully**, bountifully shall be reaping also, each according as he has proposed in his heart, not sorrowfully, nor of compulsion, for the **gleeful giver** is loved by God. Now God is able to lavish all grace on you, that, having all contentment in everything always, you may be superabounding in every good work, according as it is written, He scatters, He gives to the drudges, His righteousness remains for the eon. Now may He Who is supplying seed to the sower, and bread for food, be furnishing and multiplying your seed and be making the product of your righteousness grow, being enriched in* *everything, for all the generosity, which is producing through us thanksgiving to God, for the dispensation of this ministry not only is **replenishing the wants of the saints,** but is superabounding also through much thanksgiving, to God, through the testedness of this dispensation, glorifying God at the subjection of your avowal to the evangel of Christ, and in the **generosity of the contribution** for them and for all, and in their petition for you, longing to be acquainted with you, because of the transcendent grace of God on you* (2Corinthians 9:6-14).

"God has no need. Gifts acceptable to Him must spring from a pure motive. It is better to not give at all than to give with a heavy heart or from an unworthy motive. Extortion, whether by appeals to pride, competition, tithing or anything except the voluntary, spontaneous response to His grace, is not in keeping with His attitude toward us now. While giving should never be mercenary, in hope of some return, it is doubtless most profitable in every way. It brings immediate happiness and satisfaction and it bears a harvest in the future. The farmer who stints his seed will reap a spare crop. Many of us, in that day, will wish that we had been more bountiful in our sowing for, no doubt, the harvest will be a hundred fold. *Hilarious* is the English adaptation of the Greek word we have rendered "gleeful". One may give with cheerful resignation, but more than this is desired by the Lord. When we do it with irrepressible joy, then we come into closest communion with the God Who gave His Son and with Him gives us all. (Concordant Commentary pg. 274)

*Let him who is being instructed in the word **be contributing** to him who is instructing, **in all good things**. Be not deceived, God is not to be sneered at, for whatsoever a man may be sowing, this shall he be reaping also, for he who is sowing for his own flesh, from the flesh shall be reaping corruption, yet he who is sowing for the spirit, from the spirit shall be reaping life eonian.*

*Now we may not be despondent in ideal doing, for in due season we shall be reaping, if we do not faint. Consequently, then, as we have occasion, we are working for the good of all, yet specially for the family of faith* (Galatians 6:6-10).

*Let elders who have presided ideally be counted worthy of double honor, especially those who are toiling in word and teaching, for the scripture is saying: "A threshing ox you shall not be muzzling, and "**Worthy is the worker of his wages**"* (1Timothy 5:17,18).

Those receiving spiritual instruction are to contribute to the needs of those toiling in the word, **in all good things**. The message is clear and simple; those who spend their resources to serve themselves, can expect only rewards that quickly decay. On the other hand if we invest our resources in things of the spirit we will reap life eonian, in due season, if we faint not. The conclusion of the matter is thus; **be** *working for the good of all*, *yet specially* **for the family of faith**. Heralding the evangel requires work. This work is referred to as **sowing for the spirit!** Those who make **working for the spiritual good of all**, especially for those of the faith, a priority in life, will reap immediate happiness and satisfaction, in this life and a harvest in the future.

## Be Disposed to This One Thing

*Fill my joy full, that you may be **mutually disposed**, having mutual love, joined in soul, being disposed to one thing nothing according with faction, nor yet according with vainglory - but with humility* (Philippians 2:2,3).

*If, then, you were roused together with Christ, be seeking that which is above, where Christ is, sitting at the right hand of God. Be **disposed to that which is above,** not to that on the earth* (Colossians 3:1,2).

Many who claim to be **mutually disposed to the same thing** find it impossible to compete together for the evangel. We must conclude that one or both parties are not really **disposed to that** which is above. If two members of the body are both subject to the Head, joined in soul, they will have a mutual love for each and they should be able to work together.

*Now, being true, in love we should be making all grow into Him, Who is the Head – Christ out of Whom the entire body, being articulated together and united* (Ephesians 4:15,16).

Weymouth put it like this, *Dependent on Him, the whole body-- its various parts closely fitting and firmly **adhering to one another.** (Fitly joined together, Young's Literal)

Unresolved strife and factions only prove that vainglory is ruling and not humility, on one side, at least. Those subject to the spirit, filled with a genuine love for the Lord and His evangel will discover their greatest joy in life, competing and working together, building up the saints and sharing the good news to anyone who has not yet realized the grace of God in truth.

However, much of the onus, for our sad state of affairs must be placed on the preachers themselves. Unfortunately their competing in the faith is often not together but alone or in competition to one another. Factions and vainglory are also evidence of their pride and their desire for self-gratification. One can only assume that their main priority is to promote their own ministry. As disturbing as this is, we can however, take consolation in the fact that God uses the divisions to fulfill His purpose.

*For it must be that there are sects also among you, that those also who are qualified may be becoming apparent among you* (1Corinthians 11:19).

## Christ is Being Announced

*By every method, whether in pretense or truth, Christ is being announced, I am rejoicing in this also, and will be rejoicing* (Philippians 1:18).

It may be argued that those instrumental in causing divisions are just immature, yet sincere believers. This is possible and for this reason a novice is not to be in a position of leadership (1Timothy 3:6).

Although we are not qualified to judge the motives of those involved in schisms, we are however to make a note of them and recognize that they are enemies of the cross. And yet, even in this, we can rejoice that Christ is preached.

*There is to be a mutual disposition to be observing the elements by the same rule. Become imitators together of me, brethren, and be **noting those** who are walking thus, according as you have us for a model, for many are walking, of whom I often told you, yet now am lamenting also as I tell it, who are **enemies of the cross** of Christ, whose consummation is destruction, whose god is their bowels, (AV belly) and whose glory is in their shame, who to the terrestrial are disposed* (Philippians 3:16-20).

Being a student of the Bible or a "preacher of the gospel" does not necessarily prove one is disposed to that which is above or subject to Christ. As in the first century, the enemies of the cross are those whose god is their own bellies, so to speak, their own earthly needs and physical passions.

*Some indeed, are even heralding Christ because of envy and strife* (Philippians 1:15).

Those heralding the good news, do so for various reasons. Some are more interested in their own ministry and gathering followers to themselves than competing together in the faith of the evangel. In contrast, Paul said to the Corinthians,

*I am jealous over you with a jealousy of God. For I betroth you to one Man . . . to Christ* (2Corinthians 11:2).

To betroth is literally to CONNECT. (Concordant Keyword pg. 31) A preacher subject to Christ will also be jealous for God. His goal will be to **connect the saints of God to Christ**. A sectarian man, motivated by his own desire to succeed will not and cannot be subject to Christ, as his Head.

***Be noting those who are making dissensions*** *and snares beside the teaching which you learned, and **avoid them**, for such for our Lord Christ are not slaving, but for their own bowels, and through compliments and adulation are deluding the hearts of the innocent* (Romans 16:17).

Any preaching, regardless how eloquent, if it is not grounded in love and in accord with the evangel of grace, will invariably cause strife and division. We are not only to take notice of those causing division, we are to avoid them, also.

## The Power of Devoutness

As time goes on we know, *Wicked men and swindlers shall wax worse and worse, **deceiving and being deceived.** Now you be remaining in what you learned and verified, being aware from whom you learned it* (2Timothy 3:13-14).

We should not be surprised at swindlers out to deceive God's people. They may be confident and convincing; they themselves being deceived, believing their own lies, persuaded they have the truth. Paul was appointed by God to be an apostle, *in accord with the faith of God's chosen, and a realization of the* **truth, which accords with devoutness** (Titus 1:1). We must remain in what we learned being aware from whom we learned it. Those who have another message are imposters.

*They are avowing an acquaintance with God, yet by their acts are denying it, being abominable and stubborn, and disqualified for every good act* (:16).

*Now this know, that in the last days perilous periods will be present, for men will be selfish . . .* **fond of their own gratification** *rather than fond of God; having a form of devoutness, yet denying its power* (2Timothy 3:1-5).

It is a sign of the last days for men to be fond of their own gratification rather than fond of God. This is obvious among the "non-believers", of the world, but this passage is speaking of those having a **form of devoutness**. One can pretend to know God and reverence Him but if their acts deny it, this is an outright denial of the **power of devoutness**. A sincere reverence for God and His evangel is the confirmation that ones faith is genuine. The evangel is God's power for salvation but it is realized through devoutness.

*The era will be when they will not tolerate sound teaching, but, their hearing being tickled, they will heap up for themselves teachers* **in accord with their own desires,** (2Timothy 4:3).

Preachers of the evangel are not exempt from the temptation to serve self and please men. It is quite possible to have a form of devoutness standing in the limelight of a pulpit, and yet be denying its power in one's personal life.

## Heralding Another Jesus

*If ever we also, or a messenger out of heaven, should be bringing an evangel to you beside that which we bring to you, let him be anathema* (Galatians 1:8)!

Anathema is literally UN- PLACE, Concordant Keyword, pg. 14). To anathematize a person is to execrate them; to denounce or ban. (Webster's Dictionary)

*I fear lest somehow, as the serpent deludes Eve by its craftiness, your apprehensions should be corrupted from the **singleness and pureness which is in Christ**. For if, indeed, he who is coming is heralding another Jesus whom we do not herald, or are obtaining a different spirit, which you did not obtain, or a different evangel, which you do not receive . . . such are false apostles, fraudulent workers, being transfigured into apostles of Christ. And no marvel, for Satan himself is being transfigured into a messenger of light. It is no great thing, then, if his servants also are being transfigured as dispensers of righteousness* (2Corinthians 11:3-15).

The obvious reason preachers cannot share the pulpit with each other is because they are heralding conflicting messages. What is more surprising is that Paul lists **another Jesus, a different evangel** or a **different spirit** all together. In a recent article I read the writer claimed the **words of Jesus** in the  gospel accounts are unsound words for us because Jesus was *commissioned only to the lost sheep of the house of Israel* (Matthew 15:24). He further claimed that only the **words of the glorified Christ** given to Paul are for us today. Paul wrote,

***All scripture** is inspired by God, and **is beneficial** for teaching, for exposure, for correction, for discipline in righteousness that the man of God may be equipped, fitted out for every good act* (2Timothy 3:16,17).

Whom shall we believe?

*Let God be true, yet every man a liar* (Romans 3:4).

## The Truth is in Jesus

I realize that the context of all scripture is important but how in the world can there not be truth for us in the words of Jesus, the man Who walked the shores of Galilee? Jesus, Himself said,

*The declarations, which I have spoken to you are spirit and are life"*(John 6:63). He even declared, *"I am the Way and the Truth and the Life* (John 14:6).

Is there another "Way" to God other than by the *one Mediator of God and mankind, a Man, Christ Jesus* (1Timothy 2:5).

Did Paul disagree? I don't think so. Listen to his words.

*I am saying and attesting in the Lord: By no means are you still to be walking according as those of the nations also are walking, in the vanity of their mind, their comprehension being darkened, being estranged from the life of God because of the **ignorance** that is in them, because of the **callousness of their hearts,** who, being past feeling, in greed give themselves up with wantonness to all uncleanness as a vocation. You did not thus learn Christ, since, surely, **Him you hear,** and **by Him were taught** (according as **the truth is in Jesus**)* (Ephesians 4:17-21).

Here Paul equates **"learning Christ"** with " **truth in Jesus"**. He could have easily said " the truth  in the glorified Christ", if he wanted to make that distinction. Is preaching the Christ that Paul did, to preach a different Jesus than the One in the four gospel accounts?  Although the words of Jesus were not written directly to us of the nations they are beneficial to us for teaching, for exposure, for correction, for discipline in righteousness. Why would any child of God want to ignore the words of Jesus? The answer may be found by reading a little further in the Ephesians passage where we discover **the specific truth in Jesus** being referred to.

*Surely, Him you hear, and by Him were taught (according as the truth is in Jesus)* **to put off** *from you, as regards your* **former behavior,** *the old humanity which is corrupted in accord with its seductive desires, yet to be rejuvenated in the spirit of your mind* (:21-23).

Many preachers are afraid of offending supporters. They would rather tickle ears than to step on toes. Therefore they avoid the topic of behavior. Some go so far as to teach that we are not to judge each other in anything. Those looking for a license to do their own thing are deceived into thinking they have found it in the evangel of the grace of God. In effect they have a form of devoutness but are denying the power.

Again, I repeat, marvel not if some, under the guise of grace, herald another Jesus. *Satan himself is being transfigured into a messenger of light. It is no great thing, then, if his servants also are being* **transfigured as dispensers of righteousness.** Their end will not be according to their words of wisdom or part truths but according to their acts (2Corinthians 11:14, 15).

"A sin committed in ignorance may be condoned. A sin against law and light calls for many stripes. But a sin against grace is most heinous of all . . . Those who betray grace have no right to expect it from their fellows." (Unsearchable Riches, Volume 47, pg.56).

God's children know His voice and will not follow a stranger. They are not impressed *with the persuasive words of human wisdom, but with demonstration of spirit and of power* (1Corinthians 2:4).

*If anyone is teaching differently and is not approaching with* **sound words, even those of our Lord Jesus Christ,** *and the teaching in accord with devoutness, he is conceited, versed in nothing* (1Timothy 6:3,4).

Paul's evangel is established on sound words; some are the exact same words as those of our Lord Jesus Christ and all are in accord with devoutness. Those who teach differently he says are versed in nothing.

## You Are Not Aware of Anything

Many of God's children today, find the strife amongst believers and especially between the leaders most disturbing and also extraordinary and rightly so. The situation was no less remarkable in Jesus' day. The religious leaders were prime examples of men who claimed to be experts in the scriptures and went to extremes to appear as being righteous but inwardly their heart was far from God. Jesus had these words for them,

*Woe to you, scribes and Pharisees, hypocrites! for you are resembling the whitewashed sepulchers which outside, indeed, are* **appearing beautiful,** *yet inside they are crammed with the bones of the dead and all uncleanness. Thus you, also, outside, indeed, are* **appearing to men to be just,** *yet inside you are distended with hypocrisy and lawlessness* (Matthew 23:27,28).

Those who could quote many scriptures regarding the Messiah and the facts about His return did not recognize Him in their midst. In fact, they were most instrumental in executing Him. The problem of what to do with Jesus seems to come to a head when He raised Lazarus from the dead.

The chief priests and Pharisees were the most devout men of their day and the elite in the field of higher learning. Therefore they were the most qualified to find a solution to the problem of what to do with Jesus. A conversation between themselves, which John recorded is most enlightening.

*The chief priests and the Pharisees, then, gathered a Sanhedrin and said, "What are we doing, seeing that this man is doing many signs? If we should be leaving him thus, all will be believing in him, and the Romans will come and take away our place as well as our nation. Now a certain one of them, Caiaphas, being the chief priest of that year, said to them, "You are not aware of anything, neither are you reckoning that it is expedient for us that one man should be dying for the sake of the people and not the whole nation should perish. Now this he said, not from himself, but, being the chief priest of that year, he prophesies that Jesus was about to be dying for the sake of the nation, and not for the nation only, but that He may be gathering the scattered children of God also into one* (John 11:47-52).

It is almost unbelievable when you consider all the facts that led to this meeting. These religious leaders had witnessed many miracles performed by Jesus. The raising of Lazarus from the dead was no doubt one of the most notable because he had been in the tomb for four days. Besides the miracles they had witnessed, by their own admission, *"No mere man ever spoke as this man"* (John 7:46). These religious men, who were waiting for the coming of the Messiah, came to the conclusion that this man Jesus must die. Incredible! In fact, because of the publicity Lazarus was getting,

*The chief priests also plan that they should be killing Lazarus (12:10).*

How can men get so blind? Jesus tells us that it is a heart issue.

*I do not accept glory from man, but I know you well, and I know that **in your hearts** you do not really love God. I have come as my Father's representative, and you do not receive me. If some one else comes representing only himself, him you will receive. **How is it possible for you to believe, while you receive glory from one another** and have no desire for the glory that comes from the only God.* (John 5:41-44, Weymouth)

The heart of man cannot serve two masters. It cannot desire glory from man and God, at the same time. It was impossible for the religious leaders to believe in Jesus because their heart was seeking glory from man. Also, the fact that they were seeking man's glory above that which comes from God alone was proof that they really did not love God.

*Of the chiefs also many believe in Him, but because of the Pharisees they did not avow it, lest they may be put out of the synagogue, for **they love the glory of men rather than even the glory of God*** (John 12:42,43).

Their love for the glory of men above a love for God's glory covered their hearts with gross blindness. Caiaphas, the chief priest and therefore chairman of their meeting had this to say about his colleagues' blindness, **"you are not aware of anything!"** We cannot dismiss this statement as the opinion of a simple man. Neither should we conclude that he is any wiser than his actions dictate. He may be exaggerating to make a point but he has spoken the truth. In fact, in the same breath he prophesies the word of God, which will shortly come to pass. How amazing is that?

How is it possible that these men, after so much learning, cannot be aware of anything? The truth of the matter is that although they had crammed their heads full of scriptural facts, when it came down to a realization of the truth, in spirit, they were completely blind. In other words, their hearts were too calloused to receive and to therefore comprehend the things that really mattered; in these they were not aware of anything!

Caiaphas, himself, could not have grasped the full meaning of his own prophecy when he said, "**Jesus was about to be dying** for the sake of the nation, and not for the nation only, but **that He may be gathering the scattered children of God also into one**". Now this is remarkable; God put words of revelation truth into the mouth of this man, which he delivers, with confidence, not comprehending the hidden meaning in his own words.

Let us bring this issue a little closer to home by looking at Paul's first letter to Timothy. Immediately following his customary greeting he continues by giving this young fellow-slave of God some important instructions.

*Be charging some not to be teaching differently, nor yet to be heeding myths and endless genealogies, which are affording exactions rather than **God's administration which is in faith**. Now the consummation of the charge is love out of a clean heart and a good conscience and unfeigned faith, from which some, swerving, were turned aside into vain prating, wanting to be teachers of the law, **not apprehending** either **what they are saying, or** that concerning which **they are insisting*** (1Timothy 1:3-7).

Some herald a message that is similar to, or in part the evangel of God. If it is not birthed in love out of a **clean heart**, a **good conscience** and **unfeigned faith**, words that sound good to the ear are *a clanging cymbal* (1Corinthians 13:1), to the heart and inconsistencies will eventually surface. In Paul's day those who wanted to be teachers of law were turned aside to vain prating or endless, empty babble without purpose or use. Love alone draws the heart of God's children, for God is love.

Notice how Paul concludes his opening entreaty to Timothy.

*Wanting to be teachers of the law, not apprehending either what they are saying, or that concerning which they are insisting* (1Timothy 1:7).

Although he was speaking about those who wanted to be teachers of the law, what he says is most remarkable and applicable to our topic. He says that they, themselves **do not apprehend what they are saying, and insisting.**

Is it possible, that not unlike Caiaphas, some today are teaching revelation truth, from the scriptures, even insisting on it, and yet are not apprehending what the spirit is really saying to the heart? I think we must conclude that it is entirely possible, in any era, and the words of Jesus seem to confirm it so.

*Many will be declaring to Me in that day, 'Lord! Lord! Was it not in Your name that we prophesy, and in Your name cast out demons, and in Your name do many powerful deeds?' And then shall I be avowing to them that 'I never knew you! Depart from Me, **workers of lawlessness**!'* (Matthew 7:22,23).

## Rescued from Abnormal and Wicked Men

*Pray, brethren, concerning us, that **the word of the Lord may race and be glorified,** according as it is with you also, and that we should be **rescued from abnormal and wicked men**, for not for all is the faith* (2Thessalonians 3:1,2).

Is it not presumption to assume that God's true message will automatically be preached without the saints praying for those heralding? Like Paul, a God given, boldness is required to,

**Herald the word. Stand by it**, *opportunely, inopportunely, expose, rebuke, entreat, with all patience and teaching.* (2Timothy 4:2).

We need to pray for the saints also that they would *let the word of Christ be making its home in them* (Colossians 3:16).

The more we let the spirit of God and His word be our guide the more we may notice the crowds going in a different direction. We have no desire to follow them. There is nowhere else we can turn to. Only in the evangel of the grace of God do we behold the declarations that are spirit and life.

*His sheep are following Him, for they are acquainted with His voice. Now an outsider will they under no circumstances be following, but they will be fleeing from him, for they are not acquainted with the voice of the outsiders* (John 10:4,5).

## A Desire to Live Devoutly

*In the last days perilous periods will be present, for men will be selfish, fond of money, ostentatious, proud, calumniators, stubborn to parents, ungrateful, malign, without natural affection, implacable, adversaries, uncontrollable, fierce, averse to the good, traitors, rash, conceited, fond of their own gratification rather than fond of God;* **having a form of devoutness, yet denying its power. These, also, shun.** *For of these are those . . . always learning and yet not at any time able to come into a realization of the truth* (2Timothy 3:1-7).

Paul stated many times that the evangel is God's power for salvation to those who believe. He now speaks about **the power of devoutness**. Our reverence for God is not an outward form. It is an inward faith and awe of Him and His message of grace.

Those who have a strong desire to know Him may go through periods where they have little fellowship. As difficult as it is to be alone we are to shun those who have **a form of devoutness but deny its power**. They will hold us back from fully following our apostle and our Lord.

Paul is our pattern. The whole of his entreaty to Timothy applies to us. *You fully follow me in my teaching, motive, purpose, faith, patience, love, endurance, persecutions, sufferings* (:10,11). In most cases others will avoid us and persecute us for purposing in our heart to know Him above all else.

To **fully follow** our apostle as he followed Christ in his **motive, purpose** and **faith** is to follow our heart and has little to do with appearing religious or devout. It will involve **suffering** and requires **patience, love**, and **endurance,** because all who desire to live devoutly in Christ Jesus will be **persecuted.** It is unlikely we will be beaten or stoned. We will surely be misunderstood, misrepresented, overlooked, ridiculed and avoided. This makes our fellowship with those of like faith more precious. Not that we agree on every doctrine but our hearts are knit together by a love for Him and by the knowledge that we are one in Him.

## Love for One Another

*Now may the Lord cause you to increase and superabound in love for one another and for all, even as we also for you, to establish your hearts unblamable in holiness in front of our God and Father* (1Thessalonians 3:12,13).

A litmus test to reveal to what degree we are being established blameless in holiness is **our love** *for all who are invoking the name of the Lord out of a clean heart* (2Timothy 2:22).

*He who is saying that he is in the light and is hating his brother is a liar and is in darkness and does not know where he is going* (1John 2:9,11).

*He who is not loving his brother whom he has seen can not be loving God Whom he has not seen* (1John 4:20).

Words are cheap. Love must be demonstrated through actions. Impressive words of wisdom are not necessary to be a living expression of the evangel. A simple display of God's power through our faith and love is the confirmation that we know Him. Having all our pet doctrines down pat, neatly packaged in the recesses of our mind does not impress outsiders. The way men can tell if we are true disciples of the Lord or not, is if we have love for one another ( John 13:34,35).

*Concerning brotherly fondness, we have no need to be writing to you, for you yourselves are taught by God to be loving one another, for you are doing it also to all the brethren who are in the whole of Macedonia. Now we are entreating you, brethren, to be superabounding yet more* (1Thessalonians 4:9,10).

The ecclesia at Thessalonica, was a model group. The news of their love spread far and wide. Paul bragged about them but encouraged them to excel more in their love for one another.

*Your faith is flourishing and the love of each one of you all for one another is increasing, so that we ourselves glory in you in the ecclesias of God, for your endurance and faith in all your persecutions and the afflictions with which you are bearing* (2Thessalonians 1:3,4).

Their love was tested severely and abounded even in the midst of their persecution and affliction. Every relationship will be tested and if found true will only be strengthened by the test in those exercised by it.

## We Are All Lonely

We are all lonely, Maker —each a soul

Shut in by itself, a sundered atom of Thee.

No two yet loved themselves into a whole;

Even when we weep together we are two.

Of two to make one, which yet two shall be,

Is creation's problem, deep and true,

To which Thou only hold'st the happy, hurting clue.

(George MacDonald, 1824-1905, Diary Of An Old Soul)

One of the severest afflictions we will be called on to endure is the rejection of our close loved ones. This was the lonely path our Lord had to travel also. He told His disciples,

*Lo! the hour is coming and has come, that you should be scattered, each to his own, and you may be **leaving Me alone**. And I am not alone, for the Father is with Me* (John 16:31,32).

He also told them they must travel the same lonely road.

*If the world is hating you, know that it has hated Me first before you. If you were of the world, the world would be fond of its own. Now, seeing that you are not of the world, but I choose you*

*out of the world, therefore the world is hating you. Remember the word which I said to you, 'A slave is not greater than his lord.' If Me they persecute, you they will be persecuting also.* (John 15:18-20).

## God is Producing Us for Glory

Our loneliness, as all our afflictions, is by design. Through them our Father is producing in us a longing to be with Him.

*For in this also we are groaning, longing to be dressed in our habitation which is out of heaven, if so be that, being dressed also, we shall not be found naked. For we also, who are in the tabernacle, are groaning, being burdened, on which we are not wanting to be stripped, but to be dressed, that the mortal may be swallowed up by life* (2Corinthians 5:2-4).

To say that God allows our afflictions and our loneliness is too weak a statement. Paul said,

**He** *Who* **produces us** *for this longing is God, Who is also giving us the earnest of the spirit* (:5).

It is so good to know that our afflictions are producing for us an eonian burden of glory (4:17). More marvelous is the fact that God all along has been producing us for a longing. **God created us out of His longing to share His love.** He is producing sons who will be able to respond adequately to His love. The Greek word translated "produce" is also translated "effect" in the two texts we looked at earlier, in depth.

*Take up the panoply of God that you may be enabled to withstand in the wicked day, and having* **effected** *all, to stand* (Ephesians 6:13).

*With fear and trembling, be carrying your own salvation **into effect*** (Philippians 2:12).

God's power is producing in us an ability to stand. Our longing for Him, even if in fear and trembling, is in accord with His operation enabling us to do all we do in Christ.

We realize our afflictions are necessary; even God's discipline is a token of His love for us, not of His anger. We see the hand of God in all life's experiences producing us for this longing that has been latent in our heart our whole life. Our trials and suffering will only last a few more short years and are a necessary part of His program in preparing us to be suitable for His work in the long, glorious ages to come.

"God's afflictions are sent in mercy and directed by love. They are designed to unite us more closely to the Saviour, to wean us from the earth, to elevate our affections to that blessed world where there shall be no more pain. Every breeze of earthly sorrow is only wafting us to those high and heavenly abodes, where temporal ills are forever unknown.

Weary mariner on life's tempestuous ocean, when afflictions cloud your sky, and billows roar around you, trust in the Savior's confiding love, knowing that, like the Captain of our salvation, you must also be made perfect through suffering; and that these light and momentary afflictions are working for you a far more exceeding and eternal weight of glory!" (D.A. Harsha, 1827 – 1895, The Star of Bethlehem, A guide to the Savior)

## Saved for God's Celestial Kingdom

Like Jesus, Paul, near the end of his life, longed for someone to stand with him, but found himself all alone.

*At my first defense no one came along with me, but **all forsook me**. May it not be reckoned against them! **Yet the Lord stood beside me,** and He invigorates me, that through me the heralding may be fully discharged, and all nations should hear . . . The Lord will be rescuing me from every wicked work and will be **saving me for His celestial kingdom*** (2Timothy 4:16-18).

Paul said "all forsook me" but quickly adds "the Lord stood beside me". When we are all alone the Lord's presence is not only most welcome but most evident, also. Not that He ever leaves us; *for in Him we are living and moving and are* (Acts 17:28). In Him we live; we no longer *walk in accord with flesh but In accord with spirit* (Romans 8:4). . . *we are not in flesh, but in spirit, if so be that God's spirit is making its home in us* (:9).

If we *walk in spirit,* (Galatians 5:16) we *may be living in spirit* (:25), also and enjoy the earnest of our allotment and the expectation reserved for us in the heavens (Colossians 1:5). We can't literally go there until after we receive our heavenly bodies but that does not make it less real, even now. The spiritual realm can become more real to us than the physical and why shouldn't it. The physical world we observe is temporary, yet the spiritual realm that we see by faith is eonian (2Corinthians 4:18). There we have a more permanent homeland. It has always been there. As we glory in our expectation the things of this world grow dimmer every day.

We can expect few to understand our walk with the Lord. We may feel that our life on earth has been a complete failure, with little evidence to show we have accomplished anything of value. What a joy to understand that He will rescue us from this despair. The knowledge that He has been **saving us for His celestial kingdom** will fill our weary heart with love and joy.

## The Joy of the Lord is Our Strength

Knowing *the evangel is **God's power*** (Romans 1:16) is one thing. We desire to be **endued with all power**, *for all endurance and patience **with joy*** (Colossians 1:10,11). In a very real way,

***The joy of the Lord is our strength*** (Nehemiah 8:10).

I purposely did not cover this aspect of grace until the end; not because it is the least important but on the contrary; I have saved the best for last.

Joy and grace are so very closely related; it is difficult to separate them. The Greek word "charis" translated grace, comes from the root word "chara", literally "joy". In Ephesians 1:5, 6, Paul informs us that God,

*In love God designated us beforehand for the place of a son for Him through Christ Jesus; in accord with the **delight** of His will, for the laud of the glory of His grace, which **graces us** in the Beloved.*

The phrase "God **graces us** *in the Beloved",* literally means, God **joyizes us**. His motive in doing so, is the laud or applause of the glory of His grace. He shares His overflowing joy with us for the glory His Own grace (JOY).

Humans are equal on one point; we are sinners in desperate need of God's favor. When God opens the eyes of our heart to see our helpless state and His grace in saving us, we cannot help but cling to Him with all our might and be filled with joy unspeakable. When we realized the grace of God in truth, it was the beginning of joy for us, the recipient and the fulfillment of joy for God the Giver.

## Entering Into and Living in the Joy of the Lord

Jesus spoke in parables and often the meaning, or the moral of the story, was hidden to the hearers. In the parable of "the talents" He tells of a man going on a trip. Before he leaves he calls his slaves together and gives to each possessions to use for their master's benefit, in his long absence. The manner in which he deals with the slaves on his return is applicable to our topic.

*Approaching, the one getting the five talents brings to him another five talents, saying, "Lord, five talents you give over to me, Lo! another five talents do I gain with them." Now his lord averred to him, "Well done! good and faithful slave. Over a few were you faithful; over many will I place you. **Enter into the joy of your lord!**"* (Matthew 25:20,21).

Another slave who was given two talents also doubled his lord's wealth and received the same treatment. A third slave however, did nothing with the one talent he was given and therefore it was taken from him. Jesus then, a few verses later, summarizes the **moral of the story** with these words,

**To every one who has, more shall be given,** *and he shall have abundance; but from him who has nothing, even what he has shall be taken away* (:29).

Let us take note that the reward given to the faithful servants, besides more talents, was **entrance into the joy of the lord.** With this in mind, let us also consider what we have identified as the moral of the story, which is, "**to every one who has, more shall be given**".

In any dispensation, the reward, to those who walk faithfully, in the light they have been given, by submitting their heart in obedience, must surely be the joy of the Lord. In accord with these thoughts, Jesus told His disciples,

*According as the Father loves Me, I, also, love you. Remain in My love. If ever you should be keeping My precepts, you will be remaining in My love, according as I have kept the precepts of My Father and am remaining in His love. These things have I spoken to you, that **My joy should be remaining in you, and your joy may be filled**. This is My precept, that you be loving one another, according as I love you. Greater love than this has no one, that anyone may be laying down his soul for his friends* (John 15:9-13).

The principle that: "loving and obeying God from the heart produces the joy of the Lord" crosses all boundaries. Loving the truth, and remaining in it, means remaining in His love. Cherishing truth and His love, above all else, regardless of the cost, opens our heart so more light and love is poured in. The joy of the Lord, in the life of a believer, takes on, what may be called, a snowball effect. As this joy is received and expressed it increases many times over and matures into a steadfast anchor of the soul. It is a continual process from glory to glory. Grasping God's grace (JOY) fills us with faith and love over and over.

Grace is love energy! Love and joy are full of power; power to endure, power to be patient and to be gracious to others. Sharing this grace (Joy) begets more. By the time God accomplishes His *purpose of the eons* (Ephesians 3:11) this snowball of grace will become a steamroller of love energy that will roll over every living being celestial and terrestrial and subterranean (Philippians 2:10).

Before God began the creation process He had a secret purpose in mind, which is *in accord with His delight* (Ephesians 1:9).

*To have an administration of the complement of the eras, to **head up all in the Christ** - both that in the heavens and that on the earth in Him in Whom our lot was cast also* (:10,11).

235

## The Gratuity in Grace

*Not as the offense, **thus also** the grace. For if, by the offense of the one, the many died, much rather the grace of God and **the gratuity in grace**, which is of the One Man, Jesus Christ, to the many superabounds. And not as through one act of sinning is the gratuity. For, indeed, the judgment is out of one into condemnation, yet the grace is out of many offenses into a just award. For if, by the offense of the one, death reigns through the one, **much rather**, those obtaining the superabundance of grace and the gratuity of righteousness shall be reigning in life through the One, Jesus Christ. Consequently, then, as it was through one offense for all mankind for condemnation, thus also it is through one just award **for all mankind** for life's justifying. For even as, through the disobedience of the one man, the many* [all mankind] *were constituted sinners, thus also, through the obedience of the One, the many* [all mankind] *shall be constituted just* (Romans.5:15-19).

In the opening sentence of the passage above we see two terms that seem to contradict, "**not as**" and "**thus also**". The first is referring to the offense, and second is referring to the grace. The casual reader may just scratch his head and keep reading. To others, passages like this is a confirmation that much of the Bible does not make sense. However, those who love the truth of God's inspired word, will be motivated to dig a little deeper.

Sin, in the form of Adam's one disobedient act called "**the offense**" and "**the grace**" are being compared. There is something about the offense and the grace that is the same. It is the fact that as the offense has a **profound effect on all mankind**, thus also does grace. In this manner they are equal. Therefore as far as the offense goes, "thus also" the grace. When Paul continues with the phrase "not as", he still has the offense and the grace in mind and there is an important difference about them that he must make clear. The manner in which grace is "**not as**" the offence is found in the term, following close behind, "**much rather!**" Grace is much greater than sin. Paul reinforces this fact by telling us why,

*Yet where sin increases, **grace superexceeds** (:20).*

Adam eating from the forbidden fruit, was the ONE offense that brought the **curse of mortality on all mankind**.

*Even as through one man sin entered into the world, and through sin death, and thus **death passed through into all** mankind, on which all sinned (Romans 5:12).*

Grace is referred to as "much rather" because through **one act of obedience**, Christ takes care of the MANY offenses, once for all time, for all mankind. Grace has the power to superexceed sin, in every way. This is by God's design, and it delights Him to have it so. We cannot overemphasize the joy this brings to His heart  because it directly relates to *the evangel of the glory of the happy God*, of which Paul was entrusted (1Timothy 1:11).

*God is able to lavish all grace on us* (2Corinthians 9:8). There is a descriptive phrase in the Romans passage above that sheds light on how God lavishes His favor on all those obtaining the superabundance of grace. Not only is it God's grace that superabounds to us; so also does the "gratuity in grace".

*The grace of God and the **gratuity in grace**, which is of the One Man, Jesus Christ, to the many superabounds (Romans 5:15).*

Gratuity is literally GIVE-GUSH. It is that which is given freely. (Concordant Keyword pg.134)

Dean Hough wrote the following in the Unsearchable Riches Magazine, volume 101, on page 158.

"Grace (JOY) is favor arising from joy and bringing joy. Gratuity (GIVE-GUSH) is unstinted giving, apart from consideration of what is deserved. In our passage [Romans 5:15-17] each word [grace and gratuity] appears in two forms, grace as JOY and as JOY-effect, and gratuity as GIVE-GUSH and as GIVE-GUSH-effect. (CONCORDANT KEYWORD pp. 132-134) But the basic meaning of joy-filled favor and of unfettered giving are retained throughout, whether or not the effect of the gift is given special emphasis.

The grace and the gratuity –these terms refer specifically here to both the act of Christ and its effect. They stand for God's power-packed message concerning His Son, declaring that Christ died for our sins, was entombed and has been roused the third day (1Corinthians 15:3,4). They cover the ground of what was done by Christ (He died) and then why it was done (it was done for our sins). But the special contribution to our understanding of the evangel, provided by these two terms, is that together they lay stress on the fullness of the divine achievement and of the human inability and undeservedness. The deliverance from irreverence, unrighteousness and enmity, is God's achievement in and through His Son alone. It is not in ourselves or anything we do." (end of quote)

In the definition above, we behold grace (JOY) as favor springing from God's joy, bringing joy to us. God is the primary subject here as He is in all revelation truth. The primary theme remains His favor called grace, but now it takes on special meaning when we realize, it is favor that springs from His joy. It is not grievous for God to be gracious to us. It delights Him to share His joy. His joy-filled favor will eventually overwhelm all with faith and love. We are privileged to be a part of the firstfruit.

His grace, in the form of joy, is gratuitously given. It gushes from His heart to ours without any cause whatsoever, on our part. It is in accord with His love and is not contingent on the qualities of you and me, the recipients. From God's overflowing joy, gushes this favour. It finds its source in His desire to bless us, and to be with us, the objects of His love.

God, above all else, desires to share His vast love and joy. We may even go so far to say, If it is possible, for the Supreme Deity, the Father of our Lord Jesus Christ, to have a need, surely it is to share His love with all His creatures. This means it must be received and returned by all. This is the basis for His unrestricted giving with no scrimping. Grace must be recognized as an overflow or a gushing of His joy and His love. Any other idea will fall short and not give Him the glory due His name. Blessed be the name of our Lord!

## The Joy Lying Before Him

No other verse, that I am aware of, exemplifies the power of grace, in the form of joy, more then the following.

*Racing with endurance the contest lying before us, looking off to the Inaugurator and Perfecter of faith, Jesus, Who,* **for the joy lying before Him,** **endures a cross** *despising the shame* (Hebrews 12:1,2).

Jesus was able to endure unfathomable suffering including separation from His Father, because He looked past the cross to the joy lying ahead. The cross was His final and greatest trial. The anticipation of joy overwhelmed Him with faith and love for His Father and all creation and power to give His life as, *a sin offering for our sakes* (2Corinthians 5:21).

There is no doubt that even before His final trial He experienced a life of suffering. The prophet foretold,

*Despised is He, and shunned by men, a man of pains and knowing illness. And, as One concealing His face from us, despised is He* (Isaiah 53:3).

The writer of Hebrews tells us,

*Jesus, being a Son, learned obedience from that which He suffered. And being perfected, He became the cause of eonian salvation* (Hebrews 5:8,9).

Jesus had enjoyed a glory with His Father that we can't imagine before the world was formed (John 17:5).

*Nevertheless [He] empties Himself, taking the form of a slave, coming to be in the likeness of humanity, and, being found in fashion as a human, He humbles Himself, becoming obedient unto death, even the death of the cross* (Philippians 2:7,8).

Nothing brought Jesus more joy than pleasing His Father.

*Jesus, then, said to them again that "Whenever you should be exalting the Son of Mankind, then you will know that I am, and* **from Myself I am doing nothing,** *but, according as My Father teaches Me, these things I am speaking. And He Who sends Me is with Me. He does not leave Me alone, for* **what is pleasing to Him am I doing always** (John 8:28, 29).

## The Glory Lying Ahead For Us

Because of the evangel of Christ crucified, which is *God's power for salvation to everyone who is believing* (Romans 1:16) we can look ahead to the glory awaiting us.

*Being aware that He Who rouses the Lord Jesus will be **rousing us also,** through Jesus. . . we are not despondent, but even if our outward man is decaying, nevertheless that within us is being renewed day by day. For the momentary lightness of our affliction is producing for us a transcendently transcendent eonian* (age-during) *burden of glory* (2Corinthians 4:14-17).

*Now if the spirit of Him Who rouses Jesus from among the dead is making its home in you, He Who rouses Christ Jesus from among the dead will also be vivifying your mortal bodies because of His spirit making its home in you* (Romans 8:11).

We also look ahead, by faith, to the glory and joy lying ahead for us. As we do His spirit gives us life and power for salvation daily. This is a practical empowerment for all endurance and patience **with joy**.

It is through our Lord, Jesus Christ we have the **access** also, **by faith**, into this grace (JOY) in which we stand (Romans 5:2). Dwelling in the joy of the Lord by faith will shield us from many of the stratagems of the enemy. As Paul prayed for the Colossian ecclesia, let us pray for each other.

*We do not cease praying for you and requesting that you may be filled full with the realization of His will, in all wisdom and spiritual understanding, you to walk worthily of the Lord for all pleasing, bearing fruit in every good work, and growing in the realization of God; being endued with all power, in accord with the might of His glory, **for all endurance and patience with joy*** (Colossians 1: 9-11).

Our Lord found His greatest joy in pleasing His Father. As we race in this contest of life, let us continually look to the One Who is the source and the completion of our faith. The might of His glory operating in us will give us endurance to run the race before us with joy.

## Final Remarks to You the Reader

It seems quite unlikely that anyone would have read thus far unless, *the eyes of your heart have been enlightened to perceive what is the expectation of His calling, and the riches of the glory of the enjoyment of His allotment among the saints, and the transcendent greatness of His power for us* (Ephesians 1:18,19).

The revelation that,

*in other generations, is not made known to the sons of humanity as it was now revealed to His holy apostles and prophets:* is this, *in spirit the nations are to be joint enjoyers of an allotment, and a joint body, and joint partakers of the promise in Christ Jesus, through the evangel* (Ephesians 3:5,6).

We, the privileged few have been given eyes to see and ears to hear. However, this is the beginning not the end. If we will listen to the still small voice speaking to our hearts we will sense Him calling us to His side, away from all distractions, to be set apart for Him, and to pursue the prize of God's calling above in Christ Jesus. The prize above all others is,

*To know Him, and the power of His resurrection, and the fellowship of His sufferings, conforming to His death, if somehow* [we] *should be attaining to the resurrection that is out from among the dead* (Philippians 3:10-15).

God has provided a way to be saved daily. It is by retaining the truth of the evangel (1Corinthians 15:2). He has provided the means to stand up to the enemy's deceptions, by putting on the panoply of God (Ephesians 6:11).

Above all else, God is calling us to *obey from the heart the teaching we were given* (Romans 6:17).

*So that, my beloved, according as you always obey . . .with fear and trembling, be carrying your salvation into effect, for it is God Who is operating in you to will as well as to work for the sake of His delight (Philippians 2:12-13).*

Before Christ returns He will give His people, *in accord with the riches of His glory, to be made staunch with power, through His spirit, in the man within* (Ephesians 3:16).

*In love* [God] *designating us beforehand for the place of a son*

*for Him through Christ Jesus; in accord with the delight of His will, for the laud of the glory of His grace* (Ephesians 1:5,6).

Today is our day of salvation. It is our privilege and honor to *walk in spirit* (Galatians 5:6) and to *live in spirit* (:25).

## Amazing grace!

Twas grace that taught my heart to fear, And grace my fears relieved;

How precious did that grace appear The hour I first believed!

Thro' many dangers, toils and snares, I have already come;

Tis grace hath bro't me safe thus far And grace will lead me home. (John Newton, Amazing Grace!)

*Now may the God of peace Himself be hallowing you wholly; and may your unimpaired spirit and soul and body be kept blameless in the presence of our Lord Jesus Christ!* **Faithful is He Who is calling you, Who will be doing it also** (1Thessalonians 5:23,24).

ABOUT THE AUTHOR

Don Bast is the Canadian agent for The Concordant Publishing
Concern and for Grace and Truth Magazine. Don lives near the
small town of St. Charles in Northern Ontario, Canada. (email
address :donbast2h@gmail.com)

Made in the USA
Middletown, DE
24 May 2015